ABRAHAM LINCOLN
TRAVELED THIS WAY

THE AMERICA LINCOLN KNEW

PHOTOGRAPHY BY ROBERT SHAW   NARRATIVE BY MICHAEL BURLINGAME

My friends, I meet many friends at every place on my journey ...

SPEECH AT LAFAYETTE, INDIANA, FEBRUARY 11, 1861

Firelight
PUBLISHING
HEYWORTH, ILLINOIS

IN ASSOCIATION WITH JOHN WARNER IV

SMOKE ROLLS FROM THE CHIMNEY OF THE SAMUEL HILL HOME IN EARLY SPRING
AT NEW SALEM STATE HISTORIC SITE NEAR PETERSBURG, ILLINOIS.

This portrait of Abraham Lincoln was made by Alexander Hesler in Springfield on June 3, 1860, two weeks after receiving his party's nomination for President. Lincoln stated "That looks better and expresses me better than any I have ever seen; if it pleases the people, I am satisfied."

The Journey

ABRAHAM LINCOLN'S WORDS IN HIS HANDWRITING ARE FROM HIS THREE AUTOBIOGRAPHIES, LETTERS, TELEGRAPHS, DISPATCHES, SPEECHES, AND LECTURES. LINCOLN'S THIRD AUTOBIOGRAPHICAL SKETCH IS WRITTEN IN THIRD-PERSON PERSPECTIVE.

Preface

Looking back through the window of time, we can see a glimpse of the America Abraham Lincoln knew. Historical sites across several states tell the story of Lincoln's life in a poignant and unique way. They also recount a definitive chapter in United States history. These places embody our heritage as a free and democratic union. For many, experiencing these locations transcends time. Developing a "sense of place" is often meaningful and profound. These places connect America's past and present.

Abraham Lincoln's story began in the rugged existence of the early frontier. He spent his first twenty-seven years living among pioneers. Determined to make accomplishments in his life, Lincoln persevered to become a legendary and revered leader of our country. Lincoln was transformed in his lifetime and he transformed our nation. He became a visionary leader defined by his integrity. During his lifetime, he saw many changes in the country, both to the people and to the land.

Two and a half years before Lincoln's birth, the Lewis and Clark Expedition had returned from the first exploration to the west coast of the continent. When Abraham Lincoln was born in 1809 on the Kentucky frontier, Thomas Jefferson was President of the United States. The frontiersman Daniel Boone, who had blazed the Wilderness Road into central Kentucky, lived three hundred miles west of the Lincoln family in what would later become Missouri. There were seventeen states in the Union—all in the East.

When Abraham Lincoln's father Thomas moved the family to southern Indiana in 1816, most of the land remained unspoiled wilderness. Indiana did not become a state until later that year. This was the western frontier. Lincoln described the area—"It was a wild region, with many bears and other wild animals, still in the woods." Little remained of the Native Americans who had inhabited the area for centuries. By the 1820s, more settlers were moving into the area, attempting to farm the land.

While still living in Indiana, Lincoln made his first trip down the Mississippi River on a wooden flatboat hauling cargo to New Orleans. Floating south, he passed land bordering the river that was still part of the western territory, later to become Arkansas. This journey in 1828 at the age of nineteen was the beginning of a life full of extensive and arduous travel.

When the Thomas Lincoln family moved to Illinois in 1830, most of the state was still natural prairies, savannas, woodlands, and marshes. During Lincoln's first year living along the Sangamon River, and the following six years at New Salem, most of Illinois looked like it had for thousands of years. Lincoln would come to know the wide expanse of the tallgrass prairies and savannas very well in the years to follow.

Before settling in New Salem in 1831, Lincoln made a second journey down the Mississippi River on a flatboat. The small river village of New Salem had a population of about one hundred people, approximately the same as Chicago at that time. There were twenty-four states in the union—two states west of the Mississippi River.

During the Black Hawk War of 1832, Lincoln joined the Illinois Militia and was elected captain of his company. For almost three months he marched across northern Illinois and part of the Michigan Territory, present-day Wisconsin. After returning to New Salem, Lincoln ran for the Illinois Legislature the same year. He was unsuccessful, but was elected in his second attempt in 1834. Abraham Lincoln would be elected a representative several more times in the years to follow. At the time, Vandalia was the capital of Illinois. Lincoln traveled by stagecoach to Vandalia, a means of travel he used on trips in the following years.

In 1837, Abraham Lincoln moved to Springfield and started working as a lawyer. Lincoln began to travel the four-to-five-hundred-mile Eighth Judicial Circuit in the spring and fall of each year. He continued to travel the circuit until he was elected President in 1860, except for the two years he served in the U.S. Congress. Most of his travel was done on horseback or by horse-drawn carriage, frequently in inclement weather. Along with his steady legal work on the circuit, Lincoln traveled to many other towns across the state with his law practice and while working on political campaigns.

In his twenty years of traveling thousands of miles while crisscrossing Illinois, Lincoln saw two new technologies come to the state which forever changed the land and its communities. The first began the same year Lincoln moved to Springfield with the invention of the self-scouring steel plow. This brought vast conversion of the prairies and savannas to cropland. The second came with the steam engine. The Illinois Central Railroad began construction in 1852 and was completed in 1856. The railroads brought universal change to every corner of Illinois as they had in the East. Lincoln's "mode of conveyance", as he once described it, shifted from all horse-drawn travel to train travel. The railroads benefited Lincoln by bringing additional legal cases. The trains also saved Lincoln travel time, making long-distance trips feasible. Lincoln's train trip to the Northeast in 1859 was instrumental in his election to the presidency.

Widespread agriculture completely changed the Illinois landscape, making it difficult to find locations that resemble Lincoln's time. It has also forever altered the rivers and creeks, the original lifeline of the settlers. When Lincoln first came to Illinois, bridges did not exist. He would cross a river or creek by horse-powered ferry when one was available, but usually he had to "ford" the streams on horse or horse-drawn carriage, which in the spring could be very dangerous. Lincoln made hundreds of river crossings in the almost thirty years he lived in Illinois. Travelers on horseback in the present-day would be unable to "ford" rivers and creeks in most locations due to the deep stream erosion.

When Abraham Lincoln was elected President, there were thirty-three states—eight states west of the Mississippi River. By the time he left Springfield for Washington, D.C. to assume the presidency, the fracturing of the union had begun. Abraham Lincoln spent four very difficult years in Washington, tirelessly working to hold the country together. Thanks to his brilliant and dedicated leadership, not only did he keep the country from being torn apart, the United States was transformed into a new nation based on its true ideals.

During the Civil War, Lincoln made every attempt to ensure the war was strategically executed to end the rebellion. He traveled to hundreds of locations across four states during the war, many in Confederate territory. Lincoln took great risks to his own life by traveling to meet with his generals,

INSPECT ENEMY DEFENSES, REVIEW TROOPS, TOUR BATTLEFIELDS, AND VISIT SOLDIERS IN HOSPITALS. HE WAS PRESENT AT THE BATTLE OF FORT STEVENS, AND WITNESSED A CANNONADE AND HEAVY MUSKETRY-FIRE ENGAGEMENT AT CITY POINT. IMAGINE THE PRESIDENT OF THE UNITED STATES ON THE FRONT LINE OF A BATTLE WHILE AN ARMY IS ATTACKING WASHINGTON, D.C., FROM THE NORTH, ONLY FIVE MILES FROM THE WHITE HOUSE— ABRAHAM LINCOLN PERSONIFIED A COMMANDER-IN-CHIEF.

FROM A SMALL LOG CABIN IN THE HILLS OF KENTUCKY TO THE STATELY WHITE HOUSE, HIS JOURNEY WAS REMARKABLE AND INSPIRING. AMERICA TODAY BEARS LITTLE RESEMBLANCE TO THE COUNTRY ABRAHAM LINCOLN KNEW. THE TOWNS, CITIES, AND THE LAND LINCOLN KNEW THROUGHOUT HIS LIFETIME HAVE CHANGED DRAMATICALLY. FORTUNATELY, MANY IMPORTANT HISTORICAL SITES HAVE BEEN PRESERVED AND UNIQUE PLACES WHERE LINCOLN TRAVELED CAN STILL BE FOUND. THESE PLACES TELL THE STORY OF A HUMBLE MAN WHOSE CHARACTER AND ACCOMPLISHMENTS SAVED AND REDEFINED OUR NATION. THESE PLACES OF AMERICA'S HERITAGE ARE AN ESSENTIAL PART OF AMERICA'S FUTURE.

ROBERT SHAW

... exceeding brightness of military glory—that attractive rainbow, that rises in showers of blood—that serpent's eye, that charms to destroy ...

SPEECH IN UNITED STATES HOUSE OF REPRESENTATIVES ON THE WAR WITH MEXICO, JANUARY 12, 1848

ABOVE: THE SUNSET MINUTES AFTER THE RAINBOW, NEAR ABRAHAM LINCOLN BIRTHPLACE NATIONAL HISTORIC SITE AND HODGENVILLE, KENTUCKY.

PREVIOUS PAGES: A DOUBLE RAINBOW APPEARS AFTER A SUMMER THUNDERSTORM OVER ABRAHAM LINCOLN BIRTHPLACE NATIONAL HISTORIC SITE AND HODGENVILLE, KENTUCKY. THESE PHOTOGRAPHS WERE MADE AT A LOCATION FIVE AND A HALF MILES WEST OF HODGENVILLE.

COVER IMAGE: ABRAHAM LINCOLN SPENT MANY DAYS EACH YEAR TRAVELING PRAIRIE ROADS BY HORSE THROUGHOUT ILLINOIS. LATE SEPTEMBER IS AUTUMN ON THE NATIVE PRAIRIE. MOST ROADS WOULD HAVE LOOKED MUCH LIKE THIS LANE THROUGH SUGAR GROVE PRAIRIE NORTHEAST OF MCLEAN, ILLINOIS. THIS LOCATION IS NEAR THE OLD CIRCUIT ROAD LINCOLN TRAVELED FOR ALMOST TWENTY YEARS BETWEEN BLOOMINGTON AND LOGAN COUNTY.

END SHEET IMAGES: CLOSE-UPS OF THE LOG WALLS OF THE HENRY ONSTOT COOPER SHOP AT NEW SALEM STATE HISTORIC SITE. SIXTY PERCENT OF THE LOGS ARE THE ORIGINAL LOG WALLS THAT WERE PART OF THE ONSTOT COOPER SHOP WHICH ABRAHAM LINCOLN FREQUENTED. IT IS PROBABLY THE ONLY LOG CABIN STILL IN EXISTENCE WHICH LINCOLN VISITED.

BORN AT SINKING SPRING

I was born Feb. 12. 1809 in then Hardin county Kentucky, at a point within the now recently formed county of Larue, a mile, or a mile & a half from where Hodginsville now is.

MEMORANDUM CONCERNING HIS BIRTHPLACE, JUNE 14, 1860

On February 12, 1809, Lincoln was born at Sinking Spring Farm, an unpromising homestead of infertile ground. A leading Kentucky historian, Thomas D. Clark, aptly described it as "a place for a poet" but not for "a practical farmer who had to grub a living for a growing family from the soil." Others called it as "a sterile tract of land, almost destitute of timber," and "broken barren land." At the time of Lincoln's birth, few people lived in the neighborhood. The thirty-six-square-mile tax district surrounding the farm contained eighty-five taxpayers, forty-four slaves, and three hundred and ninety-two horses.

ABOVE: THE STONE STAIRWAY LEADING DOWN TO SINKING SPRING, THE LINCOLN FAMILY'S WATER SUPPLY, ABRAHAM LINCOLN BIRTHPLACE NATIONAL HISTORIC SITE, SOUTH OF HODGENVILLE, KENTUCKY.

FOLLOWING PAGE: SINKING SPRING IS LESS THAN ONE HUNDRED YARDS FROM THE SITE OF THE LINCOLN FAMILY'S LOG CABIN WHERE ABRAHAM LINCOLN WAS BORN.

CHILDHOOD ON KNOB CREEK

The place on Knob Creek ... I remember very well; but I was not born there. As my parents have told me, I was born on Nolin, very much nearer Hodgin's-Mill than the Knob Creek place is.   LETTER TO SAMUEL HAYCRAFT, JUNE 4, 1860

THE ROCKY KNOB CREEK FLOWS NEXT TO THE THOMAS LINCOLN FAMILY'S KNOB CREEK FARM,
ABRAHAM LINCOLN BIRTHPLACE NATIONAL HISTORIC SITE, NEAR HODGENVILLE, KENTUCKY.

When Lincoln was two years old, he moved with his family a few miles away from Sinking Spring to a farm on Knob Creek.

Remote, small, and subject to flooding, the new farm was much less desirable than the old one. Reminiscing in 1864,

Lincoln recalled: "Our farm was composed of three fields. It lay in the valley surrounded by high hills and deep gorges.

Sometimes when there came a big rain in the hills the water would come down through the gorges and spread all over the

farm. The last thing that I remember doing there was one Saturday afternoon, the other boys planted the corn in what we

called the big field; it contained seven acres, and I dropped the pumpkin seeds. I dropped two seeds every other hill and

every other row. The next Sunday morning there came a big rain in the hills, it did not rain a drop in the valley, but the

water coming down through the gorges washed ground, corn, pumpkin seeds and all clear off the field."

WILD HYDRANGEA BLOOMING IN JUNE ON KNOB CREEK WHICH RUNS ALONG THE EDGE
OF THE FIELD IN THE VALLEY THAT WAS THE LINCOLN FAMILY'S KNOB CREEK FARM.

CHILDHOOD ON KNOB CREEK

At this time his father resided on Knob-creek, on the road from Bardstown Ky. to Nashville Tenn. at a point three, or three and a half miles South or South-West of Atherton's ferry on the Rolling Fork.

THIRD AUTOBIOGRAPHY

My paternal grandfather, Abraham Lincoln, emigrated from Rockingham County, Virginia, to Kentucky, about 1781 or 2, where, a year or two later, he was killed by indians, not in battle, but by stealth, when he was laboring to open a farm in the forest.

SECOND AUTOBIOGRAPHY

The Knob Creek Farm was located amid several conical hills called "knobs." Thomas may have been drawn to the site by its proximity to a ferry and inn, which made it more appealing than the lonely barrens along Nolin Creek.

As a boy, Lincoln liked to fish and to hunt with his dog. Whenever the canine ran a rabbit into a hollow tree, Abe chopped it out with an axe. One day, he nearly drowned crossing Knob Creek on a footlog. When he lost his balance and fell in, his friend Austin Gollaher rescued him. Abe and Austin improvised their play. Whatever they did, Lincoln delighted in excelling. Later in life, Lincoln recalled Gollaher and many other Kentuckians fondly. During his presidency, he asked a resident of the Bluegrass State about his former neighbors on Knob Creek, especially Gollaher. "I would rather see Gollaher than any man living," he said.

THE AUSTIN GOLLAHER CABIN IS NEAR THE ORIGINAL LOCATION OF THE THOMAS LINCOLN FAMILY'S CABIN AT THE KNOB CREEK FARM. THE GOLLAHER CABIN REFLECTS THE CONSTRUCTION OF THE LINCOLN FAMILY'S CABIN, ABRAHAM LINCOLN BIRTHPLACE NATIONAL HISTORIC SITE, EAST OF HODGENVILLE, KENTUCKY.

THE GOLLAHER FAMILY'S CABIN WAS MOVED TO THE KNOB CREEK FARM FROM ITS ORIGINAL LOCATION ONE MILE
TO ONE AND A QUARTER MILES UP THE VALLEY. THE CABIN IS BELIEVED TO HAVE OVER HALF THE ORIGINAL LOG WALLS
AND IT IS POSSIBLE YOUNG LINCOLN VISITED THE GOLLAHERS IN THE CABIN AT THEIR FARM.

CHILDHOOD ON KNOB CREEK

My earliest recollection, however, is of the Knob Creek place.

LETTER TO SAMUEL HAYCRAFT, JUNE 4, 1860

AN EARLY MORNING FOG MOVES INTO THE VALLEY FOLLOWING HEAVY RAIN AT THE THOMAS LINCOLN FAMILY'S
KNOB CREEK FARM IN EARLY SUMMER, ABRAHAM LINCOLN BIRTHPLACE NATIONAL HISTORIC SITE, NEAR HODGENVILLE, KENTUCKY.

Heavy autumn rain in the late afternoon brings banks of fog through the hills at the Lincoln family's Knob Creek Farm section east of Hodgenville.

Growing Up a Young Man in Spencer County

We reached our new home about the time the State came into the Union. It was a wild region, with many bears and other wild animals still in the woods. There I grew up.

SECOND AUTOBIOGRAPHY

THE RECREATED THOMAS LINCOLN FAMILY'S FARMSTEAD AT LINCOLN BOYHOOD NATIONAL MEMORIAL IN SPENCER COUNTY,
INDIANA, WHERE ABRAHAM LINCOLN GREW FROM A YOUNG BOY TO A YOUNG MAN.
(NATIONAL HISTORIC LANDMARK)

When first my father settled here,
  'Twas then the frontier line:
The panther's scream, filled night with fear
  And bears preyed on the swine.

EXCERPT FROM THE POEM "THE BEAR HUNT", 1846

...upon this occasion, I mention that away back in my childhood, the earliest days of my being able to read, I got hold of a small book, such a one as few of the younger members have ever seen, "Weem's Life of Washington." I remember all the accounts there given of the battle fields and struggles for the liberties of the country, and none fixed themselves upon my imagination so deeply as the struggle here at Trenton, New-Jersey. The crossing of the river; the contest with the Hessians; the great hardships endured at that time, all fixed themselves on my memory more than any single revolutionary event; and you all know, for you have all been boys, how these early impressions last longer than any others. I recollect thinking then, boy even though I was, that there must have been something more than common that those men struggled for.

ADDRESS TO THE NEW JERSEY SENATE EN ROUTE TO THE WHITE HOUSE, FEBRUARY 21, 1861

In a brief autobiographical sketch written in 1859, Lincoln said of his years in Indiana: "It was a wild region, with many bears and other wild animals still in the woods." (In one of the few poems that Lincoln wrote he described the primitive conditions that his family encountered in Indiana: "When first my father settled here,/ 'Twas then the frontier line:/ The panther's scream, filled night with fear/ And bears preyed on the swine.") "There I grew up. There were some schools, so called; but no qualification was ever required of a teacher, beyond 'readin, writin, and cipherin,' to the Rule of Three. If a straggler supposed to understand Latin, happened to sojourn in the neighborhood, he was looked upon as a wizzard. There was absolutely nothing to excite ambition for education. Of course when I came of age I did not know much. Still somehow, I could read, write, and cipher to the Rule of Three; but that was all. I have not been to school since. The little advance I now have upon this store of education, I have picked up from time to time under the pressure of necessity. I was raised to farm work, which I continued till I was twenty-two."

Growing Up a Young Man in Spencer County

He removed from Kentucky to what is now Spencer County, Indiana, in my eighth year.

Second Autobiography

He settled in an unbroken forest;

Third Autobiography

My childhood-home I see again,
And gladden with the view;
And still as memries crowd my brain,
There's sadness in it too.
O memory! thou mid-way world
'Twixt Earth and Paradise,
Where things decayed, and loved ones lost
In dreamy shadows rise.

Excerpt from the poem "My Childhood-Home I See Again", 1846

I was raised to farm work, which I continued till I was twenty two.

Second Autobiography

In 1860, Lincoln wrote an autobiographical sketch in which he described his fourteen years in Indiana thus: "He settled in an unbroken forest; and the clearing away of surplus wood was the great task at hand. A. though very young, was large of his age, and had an axe put into his hands at once; and from that till within his twenty-third year, he was almost constantly handling that most useful instrument . . . At this place A. took an early start as a hunter, which was never much improved afterwards. (A few days before the completion of his eighth year, in the absence of his father, a flock of wild turkeys approached the new log-cabin, and A. with a rifle gun, standing inside, shot through a crack, and killed one of them. He has never since pulled a trigger on any larger game.) In the autumn of 1818 his mother died; and a year afterwards his father married Mrs. Sally Johnston, at Elizabeth-Town, Ky—a widow, with three children of her first marriage. She proved a good and kind mother to A. While here A. went to A.B.C. schools by littles. A. now thinks that the aggregate of all his schooling did not amount to one year."

Early morning light shines on a split rail fence near the Lincoln family's homesite. Abraham Lincoln lived fourteen years on the Lincoln family's farm at Lincoln Boyhood National Memorial near Gentryville.

DAYLILIES BLOOMING AT THE THOMAS LINCOLN FAMILY'S HOMESITE AT LINCOLN BOYHOOD NATIONAL MEMORIAL
IN SPENCER COUNTY, INDIANA. LINCOLN'S BOYHOOD HOME IS NOW AN ACTIVE LIVING HISTORY FARM AND MUSEUM.
(NATIONAL HISTORIC LANDMARK)

ABOVE: AN OLD OAK STANDS ON THE BANK OF THE OHIO RIVER DURING AN AUTUMN SUNRISE
AT LINCOLN FERRY PARK NEAR TROY, INDIANA.

FOLLOWING PAGE: THE OLD OAK SILHOUETTED IN THE TWILIGHT OF SUNRISE AT THE SITE WHERE ABRAHAM LINCOLN
FERRIED PEOPLE ACROSS ANDERSON CREEK WHERE IT FLOWS INTO THE OHIO RIVER.

Twentyfive years ago, I was a hired laborer. The hired laborer of yesterday, labors on his own account to-day; and will hire others to labor for him to-morrow. Advancement—improvement in condition—is the order of things in a society of equals. As Labor is the common burthen of our race, so the effort of some to shift their share of the burthen on to the shoulders of others, is the great, durable, curse of the race. . . .

Free labor has the inspiration of hope; pure slavery has no hope.

FRAGMENT ON FREE LABOR, PROBABLY SEPTEMBER 17, 1859

As an adolescent, Lincoln was hired to operate a ferry on Anderson Creek. When not shuttling passengers across that hundred-foot-wide stream, Lincoln helped with chores on a nearby farm, where he lived for several months. His most lucrative work, which earned him 31¢ a day, was butchering hogs, a task which Lincoln termed "the roughest work a young man could be made to do." One day, two men in a hurry saw Lincoln's boat and asked to be taken to a steamer on the Ohio River. He gladly agreed and rowed them to the steamboat. As they boarded that vessel, the men astounded Lincoln by throwing two silver half-dollars into his boat. Recalling this event, he said: "it was a most important incident in my life. I could scarcely credit that I, the poor boy, had earned a dollar in less than a day; that by honest work I had earned a dollar. The world seemed wider and fairer before me; I was a more hopeful and thoughtful boy from that time."

Growing Up a Young Man in Spencer County

. . . he removed to what is now Spencer County Indiana, in the autumn of 1816,
A. then being in his eighth year.

So memory will hallow all
We've known, but know no more.
Now twenty years have passed away,
Since here I bid farewell
To woods, and fields, and scenes of play
And school-mates loved so well.
Where many were, how few remain
Of old familiar things!
But seeing these to mind again
The lost and absent brings.
The friends I left that parting day—
How changed, as time has sped!
Young childhood grown, strong manhood grey,
And half of all are dead.

EXCERPT FROM THE POEM "MY CHILDHOOD-HOME I SEE AGAIN", 1846

My parents were both born in Virginia, of undistinguished families—
second families, perhaps I should say.

SECOND AUTOBIOGRAPHY

One day in 1850, Lincoln told his law partner: "All that I am or hope ever to be I get from my mother – God bless her." Regarded by some as a sentimental tribute to the woman who bore him (Nancy Hanks), that pronouncement in fact referred to the genes that she passed on to her son from her aristocratic father. Lincoln confided that his mother was "a bastard," the "daughter of a nobleman so called of Virginia. My mother's mother was poor and credulous, etc., and she was shamefully taken advantage of by the man. My mother inherited his qualities and I hers."

A SPLIT RAIL FENCE WINDS ITS WAY THROUGH THE THOMAS LINCOLN FAMILY'S FARM NEAR GENTRYVILLE.
(NATIONAL HISTORIC LANDMARK)

I went into the neighborhood in that State in which I was raised, where my mother and only sister were buried, and from which I had been absent about fifteen years.

LETTER TO ANDREW JOHNSTON, APRIL 18, 1846

Nancy Lincoln wife of Thos. Lincoln, died October 5th. 1818.
Sarah, daughter of Thos. Lincoln, wife of Aaron Grigsby, died [Jan]uary 20th. 1828.

FAMILY RECORD WRITTEN BY ABRAHAM LINCOLN IN THOMAS LINCOLN'S FAMILY BIBLE, PROBABLY 1851

In 1818, an epidemic of so-called milk sickness swept through southwest Indiana. Cows grew sick from eating weeds which contained poisonous tremetol; the disease killed the cattle and the humans who drank their infected milk. Doctors did not know what caused it nor what might cure it. In late September, Nancy Lincoln contracted the disease. If she died the way most victims did, her family in their small cabin must have been horrified as her body was convulsed with nausea, her eyes rolled, and her tongue grew large and turned red. After a few days, as death approached, she probably lay in pain, her legs spread apart, her breath growing short, her skin becoming cool and clammy, and her pulse beating ever more irregularly. Before dying, she urged Abe and Sarah to be good to one another and to their father, and to "reverence and worship God." On October 5, 1818, a week after her symptoms first appeared, she expired, unattended by a physician.

THE GRAVESITE OF ABRAHAM LINCOLN'S MOTHER, NANCY HANKS, IN THE SMALL PIONEER CEMETERY LOCATED CLOSE TO THE LINCOLN FAMILY'S FARM AT LINCOLN BOYHOOD NATIONAL MEMORIAL IN SPENCER COUNTY, INDIANA.

First Home on the Sangamon River

At twenty one I came to Illinois, and passed the first year in Macon county.

SECOND AUTOBIOGRAPHY

FIRST LIGHT ON AN OLD WHITE OAK TREE THAT STANDS OVER THE SANGAMON RIVER THE MORNING FOLLOWING
A SNOWSTORM NEAR THE SITE OF THE THOMAS LINCOLN FAMILY'S FIRST HOME IN ILLINOIS
AT LINCOLN TRAIL HOMESTEAD STATE MEMORIAL, WEST OF DECATUR, ILLINOIS.

March 1st. 1830 — A. having just completed his 21st. year, his father and family, with the families of the two daughters and sons-in law, of his step-mother, left the old homestead in Indiana, and came to Illinois.

THIRD AUTOBIOGRAPHY

On March 1, 1830, the Lincoln family began a two-week, 225-mile journey to Illinois. The roads were often so wet that they were forced to slog through mud several inches deep. When they finally reached their destination just west of Decatur, Abraham helped his father build a cabin, fence it in, and clear several acres. Conditions were primitive; deer and wolves roamed about freely. For a year Abraham lived in Macon County, where he worked for several different families, breaking prairie, raising crops, and splitting rails. (Lincoln's later reputation as a rail-splitter was well deserved.) A co-worker described Lincoln as "the toughest looking man I ever saw," a "poor boy" dressed in "pants made of flax and tow, cut tight at the ankle – his knees were both out." A friend to whom Lincoln recounted stories of his year in Macon County called that period one of the "three eras of unusual hardship and misery" in Abraham's life (the other two periods were those following the death of Nancy Hanks Lincoln in 1818 and the death of Ann Rutledge in 1835.)

HOARFROST IN THE EARLY MORNING LIGHT NEAR THE LINCOLN FAMILY'S CABIN SITE.

First Home on the Sangamon River

His father and family settled a new place on the North side of the Sangamon river, at the junction of the timber-land and prairie, about ten miles Westerly from Decatur. Here they built a log-cabin . . .

Third Autobiography

CANADA GEESE FLY WEST IN FORMATION AFTER A HEAVY SNOW COVERS THE BLUFF OVER THE SANGAMON RIVER
AT LINCOLN TRAIL HOMESTEAD STATE MEMORIAL WEST OF DECATUR, ILLINOIS.

To the Hon County Comrs. Court for the County of Macon

We the undersigned qualified voters in Decatur Precinct earnestly request your honors to change the present place of holding Elections in said Precinct from Permenius Smallwoods to the Court house in Decatur.

PETITION TO MACON COUNTY COMMISSIONERS' COURT, MAY 26, 1830
POSSIBLY THE FIRST DOCUMENT WRITTEN AND SIGNED BY LINCOLN AFTER MOVING TO ILLINOIS

They remained however, through the succeeding winter, which was the winter of the very celebrated "deep snow" of Illinois.

THIRD AUTOBIOGRAPHY

In December 1830, a blizzard dumped three feet of snow on central Illinois. Soon thereafter, a freezing rain encrusted the snow with a layer of ice. More snow soon fell. Temperatures then plunged below zero and remained there for a fortnight. In the annals of Illinois history, this season became known as the "winter of the deep snow." For two miserable months the Lincolns and their neighbors, ill-prepared for such harsh weather, huddled captive in their cabins while livestock froze and starved outside. Abraham overcame his aversion to hunting and braved the cold in search of game. The deer were easy prey because they were caught fast when their sharp hooves broke through the ice crust. One day Lincoln's feet got wet as he was crossing the Sangamon River en route to the sheriff's house; they became frostbitten as he trudged two more miles to his destination. The sheriff's wife nursed him back to health.

SNOW AND ICE COVER EVERYTHING NEAR THE LINCOLN FAMILY'S CABIN SITE ON THE SANGAMON RIVER.
ABRAHAM LINCOLN LIVED AT THIS LOCATION ALONG THE SANGAMON RIVER WEST OF DECATUR FOR ONE YEAR,
ENDURING THE HISTORICALLY INFAMOUS, THE "WINTER OF THE DEEP SNOW" OF 1830-1831.

First Home on the Sangamon River

...the[y] purchased a large canoe and came down the Sangamon river in it. THIRD AUTOBIOGRAPHY

WOODLAND PHLOX BLOOMING ALONG THE BANK OF THE SANGAMON RIVER IN EARLY SPRING AT LINCOLN TRAIL HOMESTEAD
STATE MEMORIAL, WEST OF DECATUR, ILLINOIS. IN MARCH 1831, ABRAHAM LINCOLN PASSED THIS BANK
AFTER LAUNCHING A CANOE ONTO THE SANGAMON RIVER, LEAVING HIS FAMILY, AND STRIKING OUT ON HIS OWN.

This lead to their hiring themselves to him at $12 per month, each; and getting the timber out of the trees and building a boat at old Sangamon Town on the Sangamon river, seven miles N.W. of Springfield, which boat they took to New-Orleans, substantially upon the old contract. THIRD AUTOBIOGRAPHY

While at Decatur, Lincoln accepted an offer to take a flatboat to New Orleans. In February 1831, a scamp named Denton Offutt proposed to Lincoln's cousin John Hanks that he run some goods to New Orleans. Hanks recruited Lincoln and Lincoln's stepbrother John D. Johnston to make the trip south as soon as the snow melted. In March, those three paddled a canoe from Decatur to Springfield, where Offutt confessed that he had not yet obtained a flatboat, so the first task confronting the trio would be to build one. They felled trees, floated the logs to a sawmill near Sangamotown, and managed to construct a serviceable vessel eighty feet long by eighteen feet wide. During the weeks it took to build the boat, Lincoln impressed the villagers of Sangamotown with both his gawky appearance and his agreeable wit.

LEFT: RAINDROPS COVER WOODLAND WILD GERANIUM BLOOMS, A SPRING WILDFLOWER COMMON IN LINCOLN'S TIME.

RIGHT: WOODLAND PHLOX BLOOMS IN THE BOTTOMLAND OF THE SANGAMON RIVER AT LINCOLN TRAIL HOMESTEAD STATE MEMORIAL.

First Home on the Sangamon River

This is the time and the manner of A's first entrance into Sangamon County.

THIRD AUTOBIOGRAPHY

From my peculiar circumstances, it is probable that for the last twelve months I have given as particular attention to the stage of the water in this river, as any other person in the country. In the month of March, 1831, in company with others, I commenced the building of a flat boat on the Sangamo, and finished and took her out in the course of the spring. Since that time, I have been concerned in the mill at New Salem.

FIRST CAMPAIGN ANNOUNCEMENT IN SANGAMO JOURNAL, NEW SALEM, MARCH 9, 1832

At the age of thirty-nine, Lincoln offered some sage advice to his law partner, William H. Herndon, who had complained that he and other young Whigs were being discriminated against by older Whigs. Lincoln denied the charge and urged Herndon to stop thinking of himself as a victim: "The way for a young man to rise, is to improve himself every way he can, never suspecting that any body wishes to hinder him. Allow me to assure you, that suspicion and jealousy never did help any man in any situation. There may sometimes be ungenerous attempts to keep a young man down; and they will succeed too, if he allows his mind to be diverted from its true channel to brood over the attempted injury. Cast about, and see if this feeling has not injured every person you have ever known to fall into it." By his own account, Lincoln began life outside the confines of his family home as "a strange, friendless, uneducated, penniless boy." After leaving Macon County and moving to Sangamon County, he spent five years preparing for a way of life far different from the hardscrabble existence that he had been born into. As he struggled to form a new identity, he improved himself every way he could.

ABOVE: LARGE BLOCKS OF ICE BREAK UP IN THE SANGAMON RIVER. ABRAHAM LINCOLN TRAVELED THIS STRETCH OF THE SANGAMON RIVER PAST THESE SANDSTONE BLUFFS, NORTH OF SPRINGFIELD.

PREVIOUS PAGE: THE SANDSTONE BLUFFS ON THE SANGAMON RIVER FALL INTO LATE AFTERNOON SHADOW AT RIVERSIDE PARK AND CARPENTER PARK NORTH OF SPRINGFIELD, ILLINOIS.

New Salem on the Sangamon River

Then I got to New-Salem at that time in Sangamon, now in Menard County . . .

SECOND AUTOBIOGRAPHY

ABOVE: THE SANGAMON RIVER AT LOW WATER IN LATE SUMMER, ABOUT TWO MILES UPSTREAM FROM NEW SALEM STATE HISTORIC SITE, ILLINOIS. ABRAHAM LINCOLN TRAVELED THIS STRETCH OF RIVER MANY TIMES ON SEVERAL TYPES OF BOATS, INCLUDING CANOE, WOODEN FLATBOAT, AND STEAMBOAT.

FOLLOWING PAGE: FIREPLACES BURN TO CUT THE CHILL OF THE EARLY SPRING AIR AT THE RUTLEGE TAVERN IN NEW SALEM STATE HISTORIC SITE, ILLINOIS.

To the People of Sangamo County...

Every man is said to have his peculiar ambition. Whether it be true or not, I can say for one that I have no other so great as that of being truly esteemed of my fellow men, by rendering myself worthy of their esteem. How far I shall succeed in gratifying this ambition, is yet to be developed. I am young and unknown to many of you. I was born and have ever remained in the most humble walks of life. I have no wealthy or popular relations to recommend me. My case is thrown exclusively upon the independent voters of this county, and if elected they will have conferred a favor upon me, for which I shall be unremitting in my labors to compensate. But if the good people in their wisdom shall see fit to keep me in the background, I have been too familiar with disappointments to be very much chagrined.

Your friend and fellow-citizen, A. Lincoln

LAST PARAGRAPH OF FIRST CAMPAIGN ANNOUNCEMENT IN SANGAMO JOURNAL, NEW SALEM, MARCH 9, 1832

Lincoln hoped to make the Sangamon River navigable. In 1832, when he first ran for public office, he declared: "In the month of March, 1831, in company with others, I commenced the building of a flat boat on the Sangamon, and finished and took her out in the course of the spring. . . . The principal difficulties we encountered in descending the river, were from the drifted timber." That timber was not the only obstacle impeding traffic on the Sangamon. Vincent A. Bogue, owner of a store and mill near Springfield, planned to bring a steamboat, the Talisman, up from the Illinois River to that city. In March 1832, the little vessel, on which Lincoln served as assistant pilot, proceeded upriver from Beardstown as far as Portland Landing, a few miles from Springfield. Just as things seemed favorable for a final push to the city, the water level dropped, forcing the Talisman to turn back. As it retreated slowly in the face of stiff prairie winds, the boat's cabin and upper portions were severely damaged by trees overhanging the sluggish river. By the time the ill-fated vessel reached Beardstown, it was in sad shape.

New Salem on the Sangamon River

... A. stopped indefinitely, and, for the first time, as it were, by himself at New-Salem, before mentioned. This was in July 1831.   THIRD AUTOBIOGRAPHY

A SPLIT RAIL FENCE RUNS ALONGSIDE THE HENRY ONSTOT COOPER SHOP AT LINCOLN'S NEW SALEM STATE HISTORIC SITE NEAR PETERSBURG, ILLINOIS. RECONSTRUCTION OF THE VILLAGE OF NEW SALEM BEGAN IN 1918. MUCH OF THE WORK CONTINUED THROUGH THE 1930s, WITH COMPLETION OF TWENTY-FOUR LOG CABIN HOMES AND BUSINESSES, AND TWO LOG MILLS.

Here he rapidly made acquaintances and friends.

THIRD AUTOBIOGRAPHY

From a stable in Springfield, on Wednesday, 18th inst. a large bay horse, star in his forehead, plainly marked with harness; supposed to be eight years old; had been shod all round, but is believed to have lost some of his shoes, and trots and paces. Any person who will take up said horse, and leave information at the Journal office, or with the subscriber at New-salem, shall be liberally paid for their trouble ADVERTISEMENT FOR A LOST HORSE, MARCH 26, 1836

In the summer of 1831, Lincoln settled in New Salem, which was considered an important small town, with its two dozen families, a grain and saw mill, three stores, a saloon, and a blacksmith shop. It served as a trading center for residents of several nearby settlements. New Salem was also a rough and primitive place where violence was common and even religious practices reflected the crudeness of the frontier. The village was settled largely by hard-shell Baptists from Kentucky who opposed Sunday schools and Bible societies and who devoted Saturdays to shooting matches, card games, horse racing, cock and dog fights, drinking sprees, and fisticuffs. Combatants gouged, bit, kicked, and employed any means to prevail. On Sundays, some men appeared with bruised faces while others showed up missing fingers, eyes, or ears. Instead of curbing the violence, women placed bets on fights. Strangers incautious enough to play cards lost their money and then received a beating.

LEFT: MOST FAMILIES WERE YOUNG, OFTEN IN THEIR TWENTIES—ABRAHAM LINCOLN WAS GOOD FRIENDS WITH EVERYONE.

RIGHT: BAY, A MORGAN HORSE AT NEW SALEM, IS FED A MORNING MEAL IN THE CORRAL NEXT TO THE HENRY ONSTOT HOME AND COOPER SHOP. NEW SALEM IS AN ACTIVE LIVING HISTORY VILLAGE AND MUSEUM.

New Salem on the Sangamon River

I read at New-Salem, which never had three hundred people living in it. The books, and your capacity for understanding them, are just the same in all places.

Letter to Isham Reavis, November 5, 1855

The Henry Onstot Cooper Shop at Lincoln's New Salem State Historic Site is believed to have sixty percent of the original log walls. After being moved to Petersburg in 1840, it was reconstructed at New Salem in 1922. It is the only original log cabin at New Salem and is possibly the only log cabin still in existence in which Lincoln visited.

In New Salem, Lincoln became a bookworm. If he had a few minutes spare time at the store, or, later, at the post office, he would crack open a book. He even read while walking about the village. When he boarded with the family of the village cooper, Henry Onstot, Lincoln after work would read while lying down in front of the fireplace. When Mrs. Onstot, busy preparing supper, complained that he was in her way, he replied: "Just step over me, Susan." After the meal, he would resume reading. Lincoln especially enjoyed Shakespeare's plays and the poetry of Robert Burns, William Cowper, Thomas Gray, Alexander Pope, and Lord George Gordon Byron. Burns was Lincoln's favorite. "Burns never touched a sentiment without carrying it to its ultimate expression and leaving nothing further to be said," Lincoln declared. He may well have identified with Burns, a poor farm boy who grew up loathing the drudgery and ignorance of rural life; who wrote satirical verse; who cherished company, before whom he would tell stories and recite poetry; who suffered from depression; and who carried a book with him to read whenever he could find time.

A RE-ENACTOR WORKS BY WINDOW LIGHT AND FIRELIGHT IN THE HENRY ONSTOT COOPER SHOP AT NEW SALEM. ABRAHAM LINCOLN SPENT TIME IN THIS CABIN READING BY FIRELIGHT.

New Salem on the Sangamon River

The undersigned, desirous of preserving the early history of the City of Springfield and Sangamon county, now known in a great degree only to a few "Pioneers," would suggest a meeting at the Court House on the 1st of June, of all surviving settlers who became residents of the county previous to the "winter of the deep snow," (1830-31,) for the purpose of organizing a permanent society in furtherance of this object.

CALL FOR OLD SETTLERS CONVENTION, MAY 25, 1859

When Lincoln entered New Salem in the summer of 1831, he thought of himself as "a sort of floating Drift wood" swept along by the floods that inundated the region after the "winter of the deep snow." The village offered inhabitants a chance to rise based on their talent, ability, virtue, and industry. No artificial barriers blocked anyone's way to advancement, not even a poor boy like Lincoln. In 1835, Stephen A. Douglas described social relations in frontier Illinois: "no man acknowledges another his superior unless his talents, his principles and his good conduct entitle him to that distinction." In his five years at New Salem, Lincoln took advantage of the opportunity to rise by reading books and periodicals whenever he was not occupied with the various jobs he held: store clerk, postmaster, merchant, surveyor, legislator, and jack-of-all-trades.

LEFT: THE SAMUEL HILL HOME AND THE LUKINS-FERGUSON HOME AT SUNRISE FOLLOWING A SNOWSTORM
AT LINCOLN'S NEW SALEM STATE HISTORIC SITE SOUTH OF PETERSBURG, ILLINOIS.

RIGHT: FIRELIGHT WARMS A CABIN ON A LONG WINTER NIGHT.

The Hill-McNeil Store the morning after a heavy snow at Lincoln's New Salem State Historic Site. The temperature was twelve degrees below zero at sunrise.

43

THE BLACK HAWK WAR EXPEDITION

*Then came the Black-Hawk war; and I was elected a Captain of Volunteers—
a success which gave me more pleasure than any I have had since.* SECOND AUTOBIOGRAPHY

A LIGHT RAIN FALLS ON THE ROCK RIVER AT SUNRISE, A SHORT DISTANCE UPSTREAM FROM DIXON, ILLINOIS.
ABRAHAM LINCOLN TRAVELED ALONG THIS STRETCH OF THE ROCK RIVER DURING THE BLACK HAWK WAR.

— when the Black-Hawk war of 1832 — broke out. A joined a volunteer company, and to his own surprize, was elected captain of it. He says he has not since had any success in life which gave him so much satisfaction.

THIRD AUTOBIOGRAPHY

... that said horse was turned out to graze in consequence of sufficient forage not being furnished by the United States, and was thereby lost, that said horse was lost about the tenth of May. 1832, and without any fault or negligence on the part of said Anderson. The army was marched from Dixons Ferry on Rock River, that being the point where said horse was lost, verry shortly after the loss of said horse.

AFFIDAVIT CONCERNING ISAAC ANDERSON'S LOST HORSE, JUNE 29, 1839

After the failure of the Talisman venture, Lincoln returned to New Salem, where he found the villagers excited over brewing trouble with Indians. Chief Black Hawk had led eight hundred members of the Sauk and Mesquakie tribes across the Mississippi River to reoccupy land in northern Illinois that they had earlier ceded to the U.S. Governor John Reynolds called up the militia, which sought to expel the Indians. Before the Black Hawk War would end in August, 10,000 state militiamen, aided by one third of the U.S. regular army, would spend $2,000,000 to chase several hundred Indian warriors from Illinois. Seventy-two whites and 600 to 1000 Indians were killed. That spring and summer, Lincoln served three brief tours of duty in the state militia, first as a captain and then as a private in two different units.

LEFT: A SUNRISE ON THE ROCK RIVER NEAR DIXON.   RIGHT: A MOONRISE IN THE TWILIGHT ON THE SAME STRETCH OF RIVER.

THE BLACK HAWK WAR EXPEDITION

He went to the campaign, served near three months, met the ordinary hardships of such an expedition, but was in no battle.

THIRD AUTOBIOGRAPHY

ABRAHAM LINCOLN'S MILITIA COMPANY CAMPED TWO NIGHTS AT APPLE RIVER FORT DURING THE BLACK HAWK WAR—THE FORT WAS ATTACKED TWO WEEKS LATER. THE LOCATION HAS BEEN PRESERVED AS APPLE RIVER FORT STATE HISTORIC SITE, ELIZABETH, ILLINOIS.

In 1848, as a thirty-nine-year-old U.S. congressman, Lincoln gave a speech in which he poked fun at his militia service record while he was ridiculing Democratic presidential nominee Lewis Cass. "In the days of the Black Hawk War, I fought, bled, and came away," he told his colleagues on the floor of the U.S. House of Representatives. "I was not at Stillman's defeat, but I was about as near it, as Cass was to Hull's surrender, and like him I saw the place very soon after. It is certain that I did not break my sword, for I had none to break; but I bent a musket by accident. If Gen. Cass went in advance of me in picking huckleberries, I guess I surpassed him in charges upon the wild onions. If he saw any live, fighting Indians, it was more than I did; but I had a good many bloody struggles with the musquetoes; and, although I never fainted from loss of blood, I can truly say I was often very hungry."

Despite this self-mockery, Lincoln was proud of his role in the Black Hawk War, which proved valuable financially and politically. He received $175 and forty acres of public land; gained popularity among both soldiers and civilians by his service in the war; and made friendships that would prove important for his future careers as a politician and lawyer. Though he saw no combat, he did get a taste of war, and his election as captain whetted his appetite for future electoral contests.

A SMALL GROVE OF OLD OAKS IS WHAT REMAINS OF KELLOGG'S GROVE, LOCATED ON THE OLD KELLOGG TRAIL.
THIS IS THE SITE OF THE SECOND BATTLE OF KELLOGG'S GROVE, THE LAST BATTLE OF THE BLACK HAWK WAR TO BE FOUGHT ON
ILLINOIS SOIL. ABRAHAM LINCOLN HELPED BURY THE DEAD SOLDIERS AT THIS LOCATION THE MORNING AFTER THE SMALL BATTLE.
THE GROVE IS NEXT TO A MEMORIAL AND SMALL CEMETERY AT BLACK HAWK BATTLEFIELD PARK NEAR KENT.

THE BLACK HAWK WAR EXPEDITION

Returning from the campaign, and encouraged by his great popularity among his immediate neighbors, he, the same year, ran for the Legislature . . . THIRD AUTOBIOGRAPHY

That every man may receive at least, a moderate education, and thereby be enabled to read the histories of his own and other countries, by which he may duly appreciate the value of our free institutions, appears to be an object of vital importance, even on this account alone, to say nothing of the advantages and satisfaction to be derived from all being able to read the scriptures and other works, both of a religious and moral nature, for themselves. FIRST CAMPAIGN ANNOUNCEMENT IN SANGAMO JOURNAL, NEW SALEM, MARCH 9, 1832

Upon returning to New Salem, Lincoln threw himself into a political campaign which he had decided to enter back in March.

Then he issued a lengthy announcement of his candidacy for a seat in the state legislature. As a Whig, he rejected the Jacksonian

notion that the only assertive action which the Federal government should undertake was aggressive foreign expansionism.

Whigs favored a more positive approach to governing. Lincoln argued that the "legitimate object of government is 'to do for

the people what needs to be done, but which they can not, by individual effort, do at all, or do so well, for themselves.' There

are many such things – some of them exist independently of the injustice in the world. Making and maintaining roads, bridges,

and the like; providing for the helpless young and afflicted; common schools; and disposing of deceased men's property, are

instances." In his 1832 campaign announcement, Lincoln championed government support for internal improvements which

would enable subsistence farmers to escape rural poverty by participating in the market economy. He wanted to spare others the

ox-like drudgery that rural isolation had imposed upon him and his family. To that end, he recommended affordable projects,

including measures to facilitate navigation of the Sangamon River.

The sun sets over the Illinois River in midsummer, with the river more than nine feet above flood stage. Abraham Lincoln arrived by canoe at or near this location at Riverfront Park in Havana, Illinois. Traveling with another soldier, they then walked back to New Salem. Twenty-six years later, Lincoln arrived by steamboat near this same location to give a campaign speech.

...for the East half of Lot Number five South of Main street in the first survey in the town of New-Salem...

BOND OF DAVID RUTLEDGE, JANUARY 31, 1833

LIGHT OF THE FIREPLACE AND CANDLELIGHT BRING WARMTH TO A COOL EVENING IN A CABIN AT NEW SALEM STATE HISTORIC SITE.

The West half of lot number five, North of Main Street, in the 1st survey in the town of New Salem in the county and State aforesaid together with all and singular the appurtenances thereunto belonging or in anywise appertaining thereunto . . .

MORTGAGE DRAWN FOR WILLIAM GREEN, JR. TO REUBEN RADFORD, JANUARY 15, 1833

The Surveyor of Sangamon, offered to depute to A that portion of his work which was within his part of the county. He accepted, procured a compass and chain, studied Flint, and Gibson a little, and went at it. This procured bread, and kept soul and body together.

THIRD AUTOBIOGRAPHY

New Salem's living conditions were rough. To his family in New Hampshire, one resident described the village's cabins, including those of the more prosperous farmers, as "not half so good as your old hogs pen and not any larger." Those dwellings were little better than the half-faced camps of the original pioneers. A staple of the local diet was a form of bread called corn dodgers that were "so hard that you could knock a Texas steer down with a chunk of it, or split an end board forty yards offhand." In 1834, while living in central Illinois, Stephen A. Douglas warned a friend in New York that "persons who have been accustomed to the older and more densely settled States, must expect to experience many inconveniences and perhaps I may add hardships, if they come here."

LEFT: THE SUN RISES ON A BRITTLE MORNING AT THE RUTLEDGE TAVERN.

RIGHT: THE TWILIGHT OF SUNSET BRINGS A LONG, DARK NIGHT AT NEW SALEM.

New Salem on the Sangamon River

They opened as merchants; and he says that was <u>the</u> store. . . . The store winked out.

THIRD AUTOBIOGRAPHY

THE LAST LIGHT OF THE DAY FALLS ON THE FIRST LINCOLN-BERRY STORE
AT LINCOLN'S NEW SALEM STATE HISTORIC SITE NEAR PETERSBURG, ILLINOIS.

...I remained a year as a sort of Clerk in a store. SECOND AUTOBIOGRAPHY

Shortly after Lincoln lost the August 1832 legislative election, he opened a store with a co-owner, young William Franklin Berry, the dissolute son of a Protestant minister. Frontier village merchants like Lincoln and Berry were general factotums for everyone and thus came to know what was happening in their neighborhoods. Stores often contained the post office and were gathering places for the community. Lincoln and Berry kept buying more and more stock, leaving the entrepreneurs ever deeper in debt. They extended too much credit, bought and sold goods unwisely, failed to keep items properly stocked, and invested so much money in slow-selling merchandise that their stock became an unappealing hodge podge. Eventually the business, as Lincoln put it, "winked out."

The store failed not just because the partners were overextended but also because Berry was an undisciplined, hard-drinking fellow. He neglected the store and died in 1835, apparently of tuberculosis caused by his intemperate ways. Making matters worse, Lincoln was too soft-hearted to deny any application for credit, no matter how impecunious the applicant might be. Nor could he pressure customers to pay their bills or sue them. Moreover, he lacked enthusiasm for the job and was far too likely to interrupt a transaction with a long story. He also erred in letting the bibulous Berry wait on women and in candidly warning good customers that the whiskey he sold would ruin them and that the tobacco was of poor quality. If he did not know much about the goods in the store, he would acknowledge his ignorance. When Berry died in 1835, Lincoln's debts amounted to approximately $1,100. "That debt was the greatest obstacle I have ever met in life," he told a friend.

GOODS AND MERCHANDISE OF THE FRONTIER IN THE FIRST LINCOLN-BERRY STORE AT NEW SALEM.

New Salem on the Sangamon River

He was appointed Post-master at New-Salem — the office being too insignificant, to make his politics an objection.

Third Autobiography

The Sangamon River after heavy rains near the site of the New Salem ferry. Abraham Lincoln crossed the river at or near this location frequently, at times when the river was flooding, to pick up mail in Athens.

Known all men by these presents that I John Ferguson for and in considderation of the sum of thirty five dollars have given granted bargained and sold all my right and title in and to the New Salem ferry in Sangamon County unto Alexander Trent.

BILL OF SALE FOR NEW SALEM FERRY DRAWN FOR JOHN FERGUSON, JANUARY 25, 1832

We the undersigned being appointed to view and relocate a part of the road between Sangamontown and the town of Athens—respectfully report that we have performed the duty of said appointment according to law—and that we have made the said relocation on good ground—and believe the same to be necessary and proper.

TO THE SANGAMON COUNTY COMMISSIONERS' COURT, NOVEMBER 4, 1834

Lincoln's duties as postmaster were light, for the mail came only twice a week. When picking up their letters and periodicals, customers paid the postmaster (there were no stamps in those days), and sometimes Lincoln advanced the amount due. Of a trusting nature himself, Lincoln was stung when George Spears sent a man for the mail and demanded a receipt for the payment. Lincoln obliged, but enclosed a sharply worded note: "At your request, I send you a receipt for the postage on your paper. I am some what surprised at your request. I will however comply with it. The law requires News paper postage to be paid in advance and now that I have waited a full year you choose to wound my feelings by insinuating that unless you get a receipt I will probably make you pay it again." On receiving the receipt and note, Spears immediately rode to New Salem to apologize and explain that it was his messenger he distrusted, not the postmaster.

A FOGGY MORNING ON THE TALLGRASS PRAIRIE.

New Salem on the Sangamon River

Postmaster at a very small office. FIRST AUTOBIOGRAPHY

When business took him out of the village, Lincoln delivered letters to homes, using his hat as a mailbag. Storing letters

and papers in a hat was not unusual on the frontier, and Lincoln did it for many years. He kept his accounts carefully.

After the New Salem post office closed in 1836, he had a surplus of about sixteen dollars, which he took with him when he

moved to Springfield the following year. A few months later, a postal agent approached Lincoln's friend Anson G. Henry

about the outstanding balance. Henry feared that the cash-strapped young man might not have it on hand, so he offered

to help Lincoln. But it was unnecessary, for the erstwhile postmaster had in his room all the money – in fact, the very

coins – that he had received in New Salem and which he turned over to the government agent with a simple explanation:

"I never make use of money that does not belong to me."

THE POST OFFICE IN THE COLONEL MATTHEW ROGERS BUILDING IN ATHENS. WHEN ABRAHAM LINCOLN WAS
POSTMASTER AT NEW SALEM, HE PICKED UP MAIL AT THIS SMALL POST OFFICE WHEN THE SANGAMON RIVER WAS FLOODING.

The Colonel Matthew Rogers Building is now the Long Nine Museum in Athens, Illinois.
A survey marker set by Abraham Lincoln is located in the middle of the road in front of the building.

New Salem on the Sangamon River

The election of 1834 came, and he was then elected to the Legislature by the highest vote cast for any candidate.

THIRD AUTOBIOGRAPHY

A PASSING MIDSUMMER THUNDERSTORM OVER THE ROBERT JOHNSTON HOME AT NEW SALEM.
LARGE GARDENS WERE PART OF THE SUBSISTENCE AGRICULTURE THAT WAS LIFE ON THE WESTERN FRONTIER IN THE 1830s,
LINCOLN'S NEW SALEM STATE HISTORIC SITE SOUTH OF PETERSBURG, ILLINOIS.

At an election held at the house of William F Berry in the New Salem precinct in the county of Sangamon and state of Illinois on the twenty seventh day of October in the year of our Lord one thousand eight hundred and thirty four the following named persons received the number of votes annexed to their respective names for the following described office . . .

ELECTION RETURN, OCTOBER 27, 1834
IN LINCOLN'S HANDWRITING EXCEPT FOR OTHER SIGNATURES
AND THE NOTARIZATION BY BOWLING GREEN

Because New Salem had no jail or whipping post, rowdies had little to fear if they misbehaved. When Baptists would immerse true believers in the Sangamon River, roughnecks threw logs and animal carcasses from the high bluff, yelling and screaming all the while. From that same bluff the entire community witnessed a fist fight in which a combatant was killed. The Clary's Grove Boys were the most notorious bullies. "We had hard knuckles and hot blood," said one of that gang. "We could give tough knocks and take em, without either whining or bearing malice. Ef bad blood was bred at a raising or a shooting match, it was middlin sure to be spilt afore sundown . . . . We always felt like knocking off somebody's hat, or tramping on somebody's moccasins." Although Lincoln did not share the Clary's Grove Boys' fondness for smoking, drinking, gambling, hunting, or hell-raising, he won their esteem by holding his own in a wrestling match with their leader, Jack Armstrong.

LEFT: BROOMCORN GROWS IN A LARGE GARDEN AT NEW SALEM

RIGHT: PIONEER FAMILIES IN VILLAGES LIKE NEW SALEM OFTEN HAD LARGE VEGETABLE AND SEED GARDENS.
LADIES IN THE FRONTIER VILLAGES FREQUENTLY DECORATED THEIR HOMESTEAD WITH FLOWERS
FROM THEIR FORMER HOMES, AS SEEN AT THE ISAAC BURNER HOME.

New Salem on the Sangamon River

He was now without means and out of business, but was anxious to remain with his friends who had treated him with so much generosity, especially as he had nothing elsewhere to go to.

THIRD AUTOBIOGRAPHY

THE OLD CONCORD CEMETERY, OFF THE LINCOLN TRAIL ROAD NORTH OF PETERSBURG, ILLINOIS,
IS WHERE MANY NEW SALEM FRIENDS OF ABRAHAM LINCOLN ARE BURIED.

Romantic love entered Lincoln's life in the person of Ann Rutledge, the daughter of one of his early New Salem landlords, James Rutledge. Four years younger than Lincoln, she was attractive, intelligent, and lovable. Lincoln described her as "a handsome girl," "natural and quite intellectual, though not highly educated," who "would have made a good loving wife." When visiting her family, Lincoln would cheerfully, if awkwardly, help Ann with household chores. They also studied together, poring over a copy of *Kirkham's Grammar* which he had given her. In addition, they sang songs from an anthology called "The Missouri Harmony." In early 1835, Abe and Ann evidently became engaged but decided to postpone their wedding for a year because she wished to further her education and Lincoln wanted to prepare for the bar. In August 1835, Ann became sick, probably with typhoid fever, and died. Lincoln was so distraught that friends worried that he might lose his mind or even kill himself. Tearfully he said: "I can never be reconciled to have the snow — rains & storms to beat on her grave."

THE ORIGINAL GRAVESITE OF ANN RUTLEDGE AT THE OLD CONCORD CEMETERY
WHERE ABRAHAM LINCOLN MOURNED THE LOSS OF HIS DEAR FRIEND.

ENTERING POLITICAL LIFE

The next, and three succeeding biennial elections, I was elected to the Legislature.

SECOND AUTOBIOGRAPHY

He was re-elected in 1836, 1838, and 1840.

THIRD AUTOBIOGRAPHY

THE VANDALIA STATEHOUSE NEAR SUNSET IN EARLY AUTUMN. ABRAHAM LINCOLN SERVED HERE AS A MEMBER
OF THE ILLINOIS STATE LEGISLATURE WHEN THE BUILDING WAS THE ILLINOIS CAPITOL,
VANDALIA STATEHOUSE STATE HISTORIC SITE, VANDALIA, ILLINOIS.

Mr. Chairman, this movement is exclusively the work of politicians; a set of men who have interests aside from the interests of the people, and who, to say the most of them, are, taken as a mass, at least one long step removed from honest men. I say this with the greater freedom because, being a politician myself, none can regard it as personal.

SPEECH IN THE ILLINOIS LEGISLATURE CONCERNING THE STATE BANK, JANUARY 11, 1837

In 1834, Lincoln ran again for the state legislature and this time he won. His personal qualities appealed to the voters, especially his geniality and humor. He was gifted at the art of calling on people in their homes. A good friend remembered that Lincoln "made himself pleasant and agreeable with all persons, with the rich or poor, in the stately mansion or log cabin." Dealing with the lowly, "he was respectful, deferential and sociable," and with the prosperous, "affable, agreeable, simple." He talked to the families about their hopes and prospects, about schools, farms, crops, and livestock. People felt "they had met a friend – one near as a brother." He paid attention to the children, gave them candy and nuts, and it was clear that all this "came from the natural impulses of his heart." While other home-visiting candidates would want immediately to talk about politics, Lincoln would propose a tour of the farm while supper was cooking. After the meal he would eventually involve the women and children, and regale the family with tales of his own childhood. He was folksy, congenial, and he made people feel he was one of them – a smart one of them, but one of them nonetheless. Lincoln's family-friendly campaign style worked because it was no affectation. He was genuinely fond of children.

Democratic crossover votes helped Lincoln finish among the top four in a twelve-man contest, even though he was unyielding in his devotion to Whig principles. In the two years since his first try at office he had become much better known and appreciated. A growing network of loyal friendships, many of them dating from the Black Hawk War, strengthened him. Lincoln was overjoyed. Not only was election an honor, but members of the legislature were paid four dollars a day, and he told a friend that was "more than I had ever earned in my life."

ENTERING POLITICAL LIFE

... I set out for Vandalia, where and when you first saw me.

LETTER TO MRS. ORVILLE H. BROWNING, APRIL 1, 1838

ABOVE: THE HOUSE OF REPRESENTATIVES CHAMBERS IN THE VANDALIA STATEHOUSE STATE HISTORIC SITE,
WHERE ABRAHAM LINCOLN SERVED AS A MEMBER OF THE ILLINOIS STATE LEGISLATURE IN VANDALIA, ILLINOIS.

FOLLOWING PAGE: THE VANDALIA STATEHOUSE IN THE TWILIGHT AT DUSK.

We find ourselves in the peaceful possession, of the fairest portion of the earth, as regards extent of territory, fertility of soil, and salubrity of climate. We find ourselves under the government of a system of political institutions, conducing more essentially to the ends of civil and religious liberty, than any of which the history of former times tells us. We, when mounting the stage of existence, found ourselves the legal inheritors of these fundamental blessings.

ADDRESS BEFORE THE YOUNG MEN'S LYCEUM OF SPRINGFIELD, JANUARY 27, 1838

Lincoln served four terms in the Illinois House of Representatives. During his second term, he and a colleague, Dan Stone, filed a protest against anti-abolitionist resolutions that the legislature had adopted six weeks earlier by the lopsided vote of 77-6 in the House and 18-0 in the Senate. Lincoln and Stone were part of the tiny minority who opposed the resolutions. The overwhelmingly popular resolutions declared that Illinois legislators "highly disapprove of the formation of abolition societies, and of the doctrines promulgated by them," that "the right of property in slaves is sacred to the slave-holding States by the Federal Government, and that they cannot be deprived of that right without their consent," and that "the General Government cannot abolish slavery in the District of Columbia, against the will of the citizens of said District." Lincoln wrote a protest against these resolutions which said, among other things, "that the institution of slavery is founded on both injustice and bad policy." He circulated it among his colleagues, none of whom had the nerve to sign it except for Stone, a native of Vermont. Lincoln had the document entered into the journal of the House of Representatives. To issue such a declaration was a remarkably bold gesture for 1837, when antislavery views enjoyed little popularity in central Illinois – or elsewhere in the nation. (In 1860, Lincoln said that this document "briefly defined his position on the slavery question; and so far as it goes, it was then the same that it is now.")

Sangamon County will ever be true to her best interests and never more so than in reciprocating the good feelings of the citizens of Athens and neighborhood.

A TOAST MADE AT A PUBLIC DINNER AT THE COLONEL MATTHEW ROGERS BUILDING, ATHENS, AUGUST 3, 1837

In the autumn of 1836 he obtained a law licence, and on April 15, 1837 removed to Springfield, and commenced the practice . . . THIRD AUTOBIOGRAPHY

After successfully leading the effort to persuade the General Assembly to choose Springfield as the new capital of Illinois and to pass a bill funding extensive infrastructure projects, Lincoln and the other eight members of the Sangamon County legislative delegation (collectively known as the Long Nine because they were unusually tall) celebrated their victory here. The Springfield Whig newspaper reported that at "one o'clock about one hundred and fifty gentlemen sat down to an excellent dinner." There Lincoln was toasted as "one of Nature's Noblemen" who "has fulfilled the expectations of his friends and disappointed the hopes of his enemies." Orville H. Browning, a state senator from Quincy and a close friend of Lincoln, praised the Long Nine: "It was to their judicious management, their ability, their gentlemanly deportment, their unassuming manners, their constant and untiring labor" that Springfield owed its success.

THE COLONEL MATTHEW ROGERS BUILDING ON AN AUGUST EVENING IN ATHENS, ILLINOIS.
A BANQUET WAS HELD FOR LINCOLN AND THE OTHER MEMBERS OF THE LONG NINE ON THE SECOND FLOOR OF THIS BUILDING.

The Colonel Matthew Rogers Building, now preserved as the Long Nine Museum, in the twilight at dusk.
The Rogers Building is the oldest building in Menard County—it was built in 1831, the year Lincoln moved to New Salem.

Visiting Joshua Speed

... I have had some little difficulty in determining on which to inflict the task of reading what I now feel must be a most dull and silly letter; but when I remembered that you and I were something of cronies while I was at Farmington ...

LETTER TO MARY SPEED, SEPTEMBER 27, 1841

ABRAHAM LINCOLN VISITED HIS BEST FRIEND JOSHUA SPEED AT THE SPEED FAMILY PLANTATION FOR SIX WEEKS. FARMINGTON HISTORIC PLANTATION IN LOUISVILLE, KENTUCKY, IS NOW A MUSEUM.

By the way, a fine example was presented on board the boat for contemplating the effect of condition upon human happiness. A gentleman had purchased twelve negroes in different parts of Kentucky and was taking them to a farm in the South. They were chained six and six together. A small iron clevis was around the left wrist of each, and this fastened to the main chain by a shorter one at a convenient distance from, the others; so that the negroes were strung together precisely like so many fish upon a trot-line. In this condition they were being separated forever from the scenes of their childhood, their friends, their fathers and mothers, and brothers and sisters, and many of them, from their wives and children, and going into perpetual slavery where the lash of the master is proverbially more ruthless and unrelenting than any other where;

LETTER TO MARY SPEED, SEPTEMBER 27, 1841

In the summer of 1841, when Lincoln was feeling depressed, he spent six weeks in Kentucky with his best friend, Joshua Speed, at the Speed family's stately home, Farmington, near Louisville. There his spirits revived as he enjoyed the Speeds' gracious hospitality, the luxurious appointments of a house far grander than any he had lived in, the companionship of his close friend, the maternal warmth of Speed's mother, the playfulness of Speed's older half-sister Mary, and the intellectual stimulation provided by Speed's brother James. Years later, James, who served briefly as Lincoln's attorney general during the Civil War, recalled: "I saw him daily; he sat in my office, read my books, and talked with me about his life, his reading, his studies, his aspirations." Lincoln impressed everybody at Farmington "with his intelligent, vigorous mind, strong in grasp, and original" and showed himself to be "earnest, frank, manly, and sincere in every thought and expression. The artificial was all wanting."

A VIEW FROM THE FRONT PORCH OF THE FARMINGTON HISTORIC PLANTATION.

VISITING JOSHUA SPEED

I do not think I can come to Kentucky this season. I am so poor, and make so little headway in the world, that I drop back in a month of idleness, as much as I gain in a year's rowing. I should like to visit you again. I should like to see that "sis" of yours, that was absent when I was there; tho' I suppose she would run away again, if she were to hear I was coming.

LETTER TO JOSHUA SPEED, JULY 4, 1842

I always was superstitious; and as part of my superstition, I believe God made me one of the instruments of bringing your Fanny and you together, which union, I have no doubt He had fore-ordained. Whatever he designs, he will do for me yet. "Stand still and see the salvation of the Lord" is my text just now.

LETTER TO JOSHUA SPEED, JULY 4, 1842

Joshua Speed and Lincoln disagreed about slavery. When Speed criticized Northerners for agitating the slavery issue, which, he maintained, concerned Southerners alone, Lincoln replied that Speed ought to applaud the restraint shown by him and other Free State residents who were willing to honor constitutional provisions concerning fugitive slaves and states rights. Lincoln reminded Speed of a journey the two of them had taken years earlier: "In 1841 you and I had together a tedious low-water trip, on a Steam Boat from Louisville to St. Louis. You may remember, as I well do, that from Louisville to the mouth of the Ohio there were, on board, ten or a dozen slaves, shackled together with irons. That sight was a continual torment to me; and I see something like it every time I touch the Ohio or any other slave-border. It is hardly fair for you to assume, that I have no interest in a thing which has, and continually exercises, the power of making me miserable. You ought rather to appreciate how much the great body of Northern people do crucify their feelings, in order to maintain their loyalty to the Constitution and the Union."

Above: The back of the mansion at Farmington Historic Plantation in Louisville, Kentucky.

Previous page: The mansion and surrounding buildings were the center of the Speed family hemp plantation. While visiting his close friends, Abraham Lincoln encountered slavery at the Speed family plantation.

LIVING AND WORKING IN SPRINGFIELD

During this Legislative period I had studied law, and removed to Springfield to practice it.

SECOND AUTOBIOGRAPHY

VIEW FROM THE SOUTH OF THE ABRAHAM LINCOLN FAMILY'S NEIGHBORHOOD ALONG EIGHTH STREET.
RAIN IS FALLING ON AN AUTUMN DAY, LINCOLN HOME NATIONAL HISTORIC SITE, SPRINGFIELD, ILLINOIS.
(NATIONAL HISTORIC LANDMARK)

Nothing new here, except my marrying, which to me,
is matter of profound wonder. LETTER TO SAMUEL D. MARSHALL, NOVEMBER 11, 1842

In 1842, Lincoln wed Mary Todd and two years later bought a small, one-and-a-half-story, five-room cottage where they spent the next seventeen years. The house was conveniently located at Eighth and Jackson Streets, a few blocks from Lincoln's office. Mrs. Lincoln wanted to expand the upstairs of the house into a full second story. Lincoln, who opposed the idea, allegedly had conspired with local carpenters to have an inflated estimate of the cost prepared so that he could reasonably claim that it was too expensive. In 1856, while he was out of town practicing law, Mary had the job done anyway. Upon his return to Springfield from the legal circuit, he pretended not to recognize his home, asking his neighbor: "can you tell me where old Abe Lincoln lived around these parts?" Other neighbors, anxious to see how Lincoln would react, observed his conduct with amusement. His wife, however, was not amused. "Come in, you old fool," she ordered. "Don't you know your own house when you see it?"

Mary Lincoln had decided on the addition soon after a successful tailor acquired an impressive house in their neighborhood; she was displeased that a mere tailor should have a more handsome residence than did one of the city's more eminent lawyers. John E. Roll, who had helped remodel the house in 1849, reported that "Mrs. Lincoln decided their means justified a more pretentious house." In the 1840s, a house with a two-story back was a status symbol that she "was consumed with a desire" to have. The alteration did make the house stand out, dwarfing adjacent homes. Mary Lincoln's nephew termed it "one of the more pretentious residences of Springfield." An architectural historian noted that the remodeled house was "purely transitional," blending "both the Greek Revival and the succeeding Parvenu" styles.

VIEW FROM THE NORTH OF THE ABRAHAM LINCOLN FAMILY'S HOME ALONG EIGHTH STREET IN SPRINGFIELD.

Living and Working in Springfield

We had a storm here last night which did considerable damage, the largest single instance of which, was to the Withies. A well of their brick shop building was thrown in, and, it is said destroyed ten thousand dollars worth of carriages.

LETTER TO SIMEON FRANCIS, AUGUST 4, 1860

An early spring day at the Lincoln home, Lincoln Home National Historic Site, Springfield, Illinois.
Abraham Lincoln purchased the home in 1844. It was the only home he ever owned.
(National Historic Landmark)

The Lincolns' house denoted "aristocracy" and "wealth and social position," in the view of one historian. Not all observers, however, found it imposing. In 1860, visitors from Philadelphia called it "neat," "clean, cosy and tidy-looking," "singularly quiet-looking," with "no sign of pretension anywhere visible," and "just such a home as a sensible man in one of our sensible Pennsylvania towns would care to enjoy." Some New York callers agreed, deeming the house "unpretending," "modest-looking," "very plain," "not pretentious," "just such a dwelling as a majority of the well-to-do residents of these fine western towns occupy," "the residence of an American gentleman in easy circumstances," a man who was "neither poor nor rich." In November 1860, its appearance was marred by "a broken pane of glass on each side of [the] front door, & two or three broken blinds on the side." An Illinois congressman said of Lincoln that it "was notorious that his fences were always in need of repair, his gate wanted a hinge, the grass in his yard needed cutting, and the scene around his home betrayed a reckless indifference to appearances." When another congressman called at the house in 1860, he noted that its furniture, "without pretension to show, was neat, and in admirable keeping with what is understood to be his moderate pecuniary ability. Everything tended to represent the home of a man who has battled hard with the fortunes of life, and whose hard experience has taught him to enjoy whatever of success belongs to him, rather in solid substance than in showy display." Others noted that the house was "furnished in the style usual in well-to-do educated families," with "strong, well-made furniture" designed "for use and not for show."

LEFT: THIS IS THE EARLIEST KNOWN PHOTOGRAPH OF ABRAHAM LINCOLN. THE PORTRAIT WAS MADE BY NICHOLAS SHEPHERD IN SPRINGFIELD. IT IS BELIEVED THE PORTRAIT WAS MADE IN 1846, RECENTLY AFTER LINCOLN WAS ELECTED TO THE U.S. CONGRESS.

RIGHT: THE ENTRYWAY OF LINCOLN'S HOME IN SPRINGFIELD.

LIVING AND WORKING IN SPRINGFIELD

Last evening I was much gratified by receiving and reading your letter of the 30th. of March. There is no longer any doubt that your uncle Abraham, and my grandfather was the same man. . . . I am now in my 40th. year; and I live in Springfield, Sangamon county, Illinois. LETTER TO DAVID LINCOLN, A SECOND COUSIN, APRIL 2, 1848

Mary may have paid for the $1300 expansion of the Lincolns' cottage herself. She sold an 80-acre lot that her father had left her and realized a profit of $1200. Lincoln teased her about the surprise she presented him with: "Well, Mary, you remind me of the story of the fellow who went to California and left one baby at home and when he returned three years later, found three. The fellow looked at his wife and then at the children and said, 'Well, Lizzie, for a little woman and without help, you have raised thunder amazingly.'"

Some residents of Springfield were puzzled by the remodeling job. Mrs. John Todd Stuart told her daughter, "Lincoln has commenced raising his back building two stories high. I think they will have room enough before they are done, particularly as Mary seldom ever uses what she has." (Mrs. Stuart did not like Mary Lincoln, and when asked to talk about her, refused, simply saying: "Oh, she was a Todd.") In fact, the expansion added so much space that the Lincolns took in a boarder, Stephen Smith, the brother of Mary's brother-in-law, Clark M. Smith. He slept at the Lincoln home but ate elsewhere. According to the woman whom Stephen Smith later married, the Lincolns took in a boarder "because Mr. Lincoln, riding the circuit at that time, was away from home a great deal and Mrs. Lincoln was afraid to be alone."

THE LINCOLN HOME FOLLOWING A NEW SNOW BEFORE CHRISTMAS
AT THE LINCOLN HOME NATIONAL HISTORIC SITE, SPRINGFIELD, ILLINOIS.

I have resided here, and here abouts, twenty-three years. I am forty-five years of age, and have a wife and three children, the oldest eleven years. My wife was born and raised at Lexington, Kentucky; and my connection with her has sometimes taken me there, where I have heard the older people of her relations speak of your uncle Thomas and his family.

LETTER TO JESSE LINCOLN, ABRAHAM'S GRANDFATHER WAS JESSE'S UNCLE, APRIL, 1, 1854

TWILIGHT AT THE END OF THE DAY SURROUNDS LINCOLN'S HOME AS A SNOWSTORM HITS SPRINGFIELD.
(NATIONAL HISTORIC LANDMARK)

Living and Working in Springfield

In Nov. 1842 he was married to Mary, daughter of Robert S. Todd, of Lexington, Kentucky. They have three living children, all sons — one born in 1843, one in 1850, and one in 1853. They lost one, who was born in 1846.

Third Autobiography

Abraham Lincoln's home on Eighth and Jackson Streets at the Lincoln Home National Historic Site, Springfield, Illinois. (National Historic Landmark)

Springfield, Ills. Sep. 28. 1860
Professor Gardner

Dear Sir:
Some specimens of your Soap have been used at our house and Mrs. L.
declares it is a superb article. She at the same time, protests that I have
never given sufficient attention to the "soap question" to be a competent
judge.
Yours truly A. Lincoln

LETTER TO DANIEL P. GARDNER, SEPTEMBER 28, 1860

Most houses in Springfield were landscaped carefully, with trees, shrubbery, and neat flower gardens, but the Lincolns did little to improve the appearance of their grounds. Mary Lincoln's eldest sister recalled that neither Mary nor Abraham "loved the beautiful – I have planted flowers in their front yard myself to hide nakedness – ugliness &c. &c. have done it often – and often – Mrs Lincoln never planted trees – Roses – never made a garden, at least not more than once or twice." A next-door neighbor remembered that "Lincoln was a poor landscape gardener and his yard was graced by very little shrubbery. He once decided to plant some rosebushes in the yard, and called my attention to them, but in a short time he had forgotten all about them." Lincoln, this neighbor added, "never planted any vines or trees of any kind; in fact seemed to take little, if any, interest in things of that kind. Finally, however, yielding to my oft-repeated suggestion, he undertook to cultivate a garden in the yard in back of his house; but one season's experience in caring for his flowers and vegetables sufficed to cure him of all desire for another." The house's bare appearance moved one observer to criticize its "almost unbecoming absence of taste and refinement."

LEFT: THIS PORTRAIT OF ABRAHAM LINCOLN WAS MADE BY WILLIAM SHAW IN SPRINGFIELD DURING THE SUMMER OF 1860.

RIGHT: THE ORIGINAL BANISTER IN THE ENTRYWAY AT LINCOLN'S HOME IS STILL IN USE.

From 1849 to 1854, both inclusive, practiced law more assiduously than ever before.

SECOND AUTOBIOGRAPHY

ABRAHAM LINCOLN HAD OFFICES ON THE SECOND AND THIRD FLOOR OF THIS BUILDING ON SPRINGFIELD'S TOWN SQUARE,
LINCOLN-HERNDON LAW OFFICES STATE HISTORIC SITE ON THE CENTRAL SQUARE IN SPRINGFIELD, ILLINOIS.

After the election he borrowed books of Stuart, took them home with him, and went at it in good earnest. He studied with nobody.

The Lincoln-Herndon law offices, which Lincoln and his third partner William H. Herndon occupied from 1843 to about 1852, are located across from the Old State Capitol. For a short while, Lincoln and his second partner, Stephen T. Logan, also used these premises. Other occupants of this building included the Illinois federal court, the local post office, and additional attorneys. Lincoln's offices were meagerly furnished with a plain small desk and table, a couch, and a few wooden chairs. The floors were so seldom cleaned that plants took root in the accumulated dirt. As a congressman (1847-49), Lincoln had distributed seeds to his farmer constituents; from some of the packets that he had brought home from Washington the contents leaked out and sprouted in the office. The windows were also filthy. The upper and center panels of the office door leading to the hallway were missing, and any nimble visitor could easily have climbed through it. In a crude bookcase stood few books, for Lincoln and Herndon made frequent use of the well-stocked law library at the capitol. Henry C. Whitney thought that "no lawyer's office could have been more unkempt, untidy and uninviting." The Lincoln-Herndon partnership, formed in 1844 and lasting till Lincoln departed Springfield in 1861, was harmonious. The two men "never had a cross word – a quarrel nor any misunderstandings – however small." When other lawyers tried to supplant Herndon, Lincoln rebuffed their overtures. Herndon's fondness for liquor often landed him in trouble and embarrassed his partner, who characteristically overlooked this foible. Herndon said "in his treatment of me Mr. Lincoln was the most generous, forbearing, and charitable man I ever knew. Often though I yielded to temptation he invariably refrained from joining in the popular denunciation which, though not unmerited, was so frequently heaped upon me. He never chided, never censured, never criticized my conduct."

ABRAHAM LINCOLN RENTED THREE DIFFERENT OFFICES OVER NINE YEARS IN THIS BUILDING. HE WAS IN THE OFFICE ON THE LEFT FOR FIVE YEARS AND THE OFFICE ON THE RIGHT FOR ONE YEAR. LINCOLN OFTEN WORKED BY THE WINDOWS FOR MORE LIGHT.

Living and Working in Springfield

That "union is strength" is a truth that has been known, illustrated and declared, in various ways and forms in all ages of the world. That great fabulist and philosopher, Aesop, illustrated it by his fable of the bundle of sticks; and he whose wisdom surpasses that of all philosophers, has declared that "a house divided against itself cannot stand."

CAMPAIGN CIRCULAR FROM WHIG COMMITTEE, SPRINGFIELD, MARCH 4, 1843

THE LAST LIGHT OF AN EARLY AUTUMN DAY FALLS ON THE OLD STATE CAPITOL STATE HISTORIC SITE WHERE ABRAHAM LINCOLN VISITED REGULARLY FOR ALMOST TWENTY YEARS. THE CORNERSTONE FOR THE OLD STATE CAPITOL WAS LAID JULY 4, 1837, AND THE BUILDING WAS CONSTRUCTED FROM A LOCALLY-QUARRIED DOLOMITE. (NATIONAL HISTORIC LANDMARK)

We have to fight this battle upon principle, and upon principle alone.

SPEECH AT SPRINGFIELD, JULY 17, 1858

In the 1840s, Lincoln averaged about forty Supreme Court cases annually until the fall of 1847, when he left Illinois to serve in Congress. In the 1850s, he had fewer cases, but they involved higher stakes. Of the 5,173 documented cases that he and his partners participated in, 411 were tried in the Illinois Supreme Court. All of them were civil rather than criminal cases, primarily involving the ownership of horses and other animals. Lawyers practicing far from Springfield regularly asked Lincoln to handle cases they wished to appeal to the Illinois Supreme Court. Just after he returned from Congress in 1849, that tribunal, which had been meeting exclusively in Springfield, began holding sessions at Ottawa and Mt. Vernon as well as at the capital. Now and then, Lincoln would attend Supreme Court sessions in Ottawa, but most of his work before that body took place in Springfield.

On the evening of June 16, 1858, Lincoln delivered one of his most famous speeches in the Hall of Representatives, where he uncharacteristically read from a manuscript. He had just been nominated by the Republican state convention as their candidate to run against Stephen A. Douglas for the U.S. Senate. Lincoln had been working steadily on his speech for over a week, taking great pains to make it accurate. He "delivered it as if he had weighed every word," fully aware of "the weight of the startling conclusions to which his unerring logic had led him." Lincoln aimed to show that Douglas's rebellion against President James Buchanan, which rendered the Little Giant so attractive to many opponents of slavery, was merely superficial and that the Senator and the President fundamentally agreed on basic principles and had cooperated, either by design or coincidence, in promoting the interests of the slaveholding South.

THE ILLINOIS SUPREME COURT WHERE ABRAHAM LINCOLN TRIED MANY CASES AT THE OLD STATE CAPITOL STATE HISTORIC SITE IN SPRINGFIELD, ILLINOIS. LINCOLN WAS INFLUENTIAL IN BRINGING THE CAPITAL TO SPRINGFIELD.

Our cause, then, must be intrusted to, and conducted by its own undoubted friends— those whose hands are free, whose hearts are in the work—who do care for the result.... The result is not doubtful. We shall not fail—if we stand firm, we shall not fail.

"A HOUSE DIVIDED" SPEECH, SPRINGFIELD, JUNE 16, 1858

"A house divided against itself cannot stand."

I believe this government cannot endure, permanently half slave and half free.

I do not expect the Union to be dissolved—I do not expect the house to fall—but I do expect it will cease to be divided.

It will become all one thing, or all the other.

"A HOUSE DIVIDED" SPEECH, SPRINGFIELD, JUNE 16, 1858

Lincoln began with a paraphrase of what he considered "the very best speech ever delivered," Daniel Webster's second reply to Senator Robert Y. Hayne in 1830. "If we could first know where we are, and whither we are tending, we could then better judge what to do, and how to do it." Since 1854, when Senator Douglas had introduced the Kansas-Nebraska Act, a measure "with the avowed object, and confident promise of putting an end to slavery agitation," that agitation "has not only, not ceased, but has constantly augmented." Such agitation, Lincoln predicted, "will not cease, until a crisis shall have been reached, and passed." That was inevitable, he said, because a "house divided against itself cannot stand," as Jesus had long ago warned. "I believe this government cannot endure, permanently half slave and half free. I do not expect the Union to be dissolved – I do not expect the house to fall – but I do expect it will cease to be divided. It will become all one thing, or all the other. Either the opponents of slavery, will arrest the further spread of it, and place it where the public mind shall rest in the belief that it is in course of ultimate extinction; or its advocates will push it forward, till it shall become alike lawful in all the States, old as well as new – North as well as South."

THE HOUSE OF REPRESENTATIVES HALL IN THE OLD STATE CAPITOL STATE HISTORIC SITE, SPRINGFIELD, ILLINOIS.

From the balcony of the House of Representatives Hall in the Old State Capitol where Abraham Lincoln delivered several speeches including his "A House Divided" Speech. (National Historic Landmark)

All our friends—they are too numerous to be now named individually, while there is no one of them who is not too dear to be forgotten or neglected.

A TOAST VOLUNTEERED AT A PUBLIC DINNER AT SPRINGFIELD, JULY 25, 1837

ABRAHAM AND MARY LINCOLN ATTENDED SOCIAL GATHERINGS AT BENJAMIN AND HELEN EDWARDS'S HOME,
THE OLDEST HOME IN SPRINGFIELD ON ITS ORIGINAL FOUNDATION, EDWARDS PLACE HISTORIC HOME IN SPRINGFIELD, ILLINOIS.

How miserably things seem to be arranged in this world. If we have no friends, we have no pleasure; and if we have them, we are sure to lose them, and be doubly pained by the loss. LETTER TO JOSHUA SPEED, FEBRUARY 25, 1842

. . . intensity of thought, which will some times wear the sweetest idea thread-bare and turn it to the bitterness of death. LETTER TO JOSHUA SPEED, ON OR SLIGHTLY BEFORE JANUARY 3, 1842

. . . the noblest work of God—an honest man. EULOGY ON BENJAMIN FERGUSON, FEBRUARY 8, 1842

Benjamin and Helen Dodge Edwards met Mary Todd soon after they arrived in Springfield in 1840, while guests at the home of Mary's sister. Their own home became the heart of Springfield's early social and political life, occasionally hosting Abraham and Mary. Helen and Mary maintained a lifelong friendship. The Edwardses were among the close circle of friends present at the Lincoln's marriage in 1842. According to Mrs. Edwards, "the wedding guests were few, not more than thirty, for it was not much more than a family gathering; only two or three of Mary Todd's young friends were present. The 'entertainment' was simple, but in beautiful taste, but the bride had neither veil nor flowers in her hair. There had been no elaborate trousseau, for the bride of the future President of the United States, nor even a handsome wedding gown, nor was it a gay wedding." Mrs. Edwards detected little love between the bride and groom. "I have often doubted," she later wrote, "that it was really a love affair." Mrs. Edwards believed that Lincoln's marriage to Mary Todd was a match "made up" by "mutual friends." Lincoln, she reported, "was deeply in love with Matilda Edwards, a daughter of Mr. Cyrus Edwards."

REDBUD TREES IN BLOOM AT THE EDWARDS PLACE HISTORIC HOME, NOW A MUSEUM AND HOME TO THE SPRINGFIELD ART ASSOCIATION.

ABRAHAM LINCOLN WAS A GUEST HERE WHEN THIS WAS THE HOME OF ROBERT IRWIN. NOW A MUSEUM, THE ELIJAH ILES HOUSE IS THE OLDEST HOME IN SPRINGFIELD. IT IS LOCATED ABOUT ONE HALF BLOCK FROM ITS ORIGINAL LOCATION.

... he is hereby authorized to purchase a suitable house and lot, within the town of Springfield, for a residence for the Governor of the state ...

BILL INTRODUCED IN ILLINOIS LEGISLATURE, JANUARY 24, 1840

The Elijah Iles House is Springfield's oldest house, dating back to circa 1837. Iles, one of the town's founders, sold it to Robert Irwin, who was Lincoln's banker and close friend. In 1861, when Irwin urged the appointment of an unsavory character (a partner of Irwin's son-in-law) to a lucrative government post, Secretary of the Treasury Salmon Chase objected. Lincoln explained that he supported the nomination at "the urgent solicitation of an old friend who has served me all my life, and who has never before received or asked anything in return." Despite the treasury secretary's misgivings, the appointment was made and turned out to be a serious embarrassment, for the gentleman in question proved to be corrupt as well as inefficient.

BUILT IN 1855, THE ILLINOIS EXECUTIVE MANSION IS ONE OF THE THREE OLDEST GOVERNOR'S RESIDENCES HAVING CONTINUOUS USE IN THE UNITED STATES AND THE MANSION IS A HISTORICAL MUSEUM. ABRAHAM LINCOLN FREQUENTLY VISITED THE EXECUTIVE MANSION IN SPRINGFIELD, ILLINOIS.

FOLLOWING THE EIGHTH JUDICIAL CIRCUIT

I am following the circuit and shall be at Bloomington, Ills., two weeks, ending on the 24th of this month . . .

LETTER TO LEWIS M. HAYS, SEPTEMBER 8, 1853

ABRAHAM LINCOLN SPENT MANY DAYS EACH YEAR TRAVELING PRAIRIE ROADS BY HORSE THROUGHOUT ILLINOIS.
LATE SEPTEMBER IS AUTUMN ON THE NATIVE PRAIRIE. MOST ROADS WOULD HAVE LOOKED MUCH LIKE THIS LANE
THROUGH SUGAR GROVE PRAIRIE NORTHEAST OF MCLEAN, ILLINOIS. THIS LOCATION IS NEAR THE OLD CIRCUIT ROAD
LINCOLN TRAVELED FOR ALMOST TWENTY YEARS BETWEEN BLOOMINGTON AND LOGAN COUNTY.

The probability that we may fall in the struggle ought not to deter us from the support of a cause we believe to be just; it shall not deter me.

SPEECH ON THE SUB-TREASURY, DECEMBER [26], 1839

Lincoln and his partners could not make ends meet if they confined their practice to Springfield, so, like most of their colleagues, they rode the circuit each spring and fall. When Lincoln began practicing law in 1837, the First Judicial Circuit encompassed ten counties. In 1839, when Sangamon County was included in the newly-created Eighth Judicial Circuit, Lincoln traveled its nine counties but did the bulk of his firm's work in Sangamon, Tazewell, Logan, and McLean Counties. Judge Thomas Drummond considered Lincoln among "the most successful jury lawyers we have ever had in the State [of Illinois]," and fellow attorney Henry C. Whitney recalled that Lincoln offered "clear statements of his facts and points, and argued his cases with great force and frequently with aggressiveness and pugnacity." In the "rough-and-tumble practice on the circuit, where advocacy was relied on rather than exact knowledge or application of legal principles," Lincoln was "especially effective." Another colleague at the bar, Orlando B. Ficklin, reported that Lincoln "was a strong, sensible speaker, of keen discernment, and was at his best before a jury. He could present his points in a stately array. He had a fashion of pointing at the jury with his long bony forefinger of his right hand. There seemed to be something magnetic always about that finger." That digit seemed to ask, "Don't you see?" Lincoln's close friend, attorney Leonard Swett, judged that Lincoln as a trial lawyer "had few equals and no superiors. He was as hard a man to beat in a closely contested case as I have ever met. He was wise in knowing what to attempt and what to let alone. . . . He was wise as a serpent in the trial of a case, but I tell you I have got too many scars from his blows to certify that he was harmless as a dove."

PRAIRIE GRASSES SILHOUETTED IN THE TWILIGHT OF AN AUTUMN SUNSET.

Following the Eighth Judicial Circuit

We the undersigned being appointed to view and locate a road.
Begining at Musick's ferry on Salt Creek.

To the County Commissioners' Court, June [2], 1834

THE ROUGH DIRT ROADS ACROSS THE PRAIRIES WERE OFTEN EITHER DUSTY OR MUDDY, AS THIS DIRT LANE THROUGH
SUGAR GROVE PRAIRIE NORTHEAST OF MCLEAN, ILLINOIS. THIS LOCATION IS NEAR THE OLD CIRCUIT ROAD
LINCOLN TRAVELED BETWEEN BLOOMINGTON AND LOGAN COUNTY.

Woodland phlox blooming at or near the site of Musick's Ferry on Salt Creek, north of Middletown, Illinois. Abraham Lincoln crossed Salt Creek traveling north on the old Eighth Judicial Circuit road.

Following the Eighth Judicial Circuit

We, the undersigned, citizens of Sangamon county respectfully request, that your Honorable body will pass an order for the establishment of a county road to commence at Middletown near Musick's bridge. Thence the nearest and best rout to Meaddows' Mill at the Sugar Grove. PETITION TO COUNTY COURT, NOVEMBER 30, 1836

THE MIDDLETOWN STAGECOACH INN, ALSO CALLED THE DUNLAP HOUSE, IN MIDDLETOWN, ILLINOIS,
WAS THE FIRST STAGE STOP NORTH FROM SPRINGFIELD ON THE OLD SPRINGFIELD-PEORIA ROAD.
ABRAHAM LINCOLN STOPPED HERE AS HE TRAVELED NORTH FOLLOWING THE CIRCUIT. NOW A MUSEUM,
IT IS THE OLDEST AND POSSIBLY THE ONLY WOODEN STAGECOACH INN REMAINING IN ILLINOIS.

This is a world of compensations; and he who would be no slave, must consent to have no slave. Those who deny freedom to others, deserve it not for themselves; and, under a just God, can not long retain it. LETTER TO HENRY L. PIERCE AND OTHERS, APRIL 6, 1859

In Middletown, members of the Illinois General Assembly often stayed overnight at the Stagecoach Inn as they traveled the route between Peoria and Springfield. On at least two occasions, Lincoln was a guest at the inn, which today is the oldest such wooden structure in the state. In 1837, George W. Dunlap was licensed to keep a tavern at Middletown. He was authorized to charge twenty-five cents for meals, twelve and a half cents for overnight lodging, and twenty-five cents for stabling a horse overnight. Just after the Civil War, the inn was removed to the nearby countryside. In 1986, the 85-ton building was returned to downtown Middletown, and in 2001 it was opened to the public as a historic site.

THE MIDDLETOWN LIBRARY IS THE OLDEST BRICK BUILDING IN LOGAN COUNTY. IT WAS THE KNAPP STORE AND MIDDLETOWN POST OFFICE IN 1840. ABRAHAM LINCOLN TRAVELED PAST THIS BUILDING MANY TIMES FOLLOWING THE CIRCUIT.

Following the Eighth Judicial Circuit

When I shall reach Tremont, we will talk over every thing at large.

LETTER TO BENJAMIN F. JAMES, JANUARY 14, 1846

THE SUN SETS OVER A PEACEFUL SUGAR CREEK ON A SEPTEMBER EVENING. ABRAHAM LINCOLN CROSSED SUGAR CREEK
WHILE TRAVELING THE CIRCUIT ON THE OLD SPRINGFIELD-PEORIA ROAD AT OR NEAR THIS LOCATION
BETWEEN MIDDLETOWN AND NEW HOLLAND, ILLINOIS.

Dont you remember . . . swiming your horses over the Mackinaw on the trip?

LETTER TO JOSEPHUS HEWETT, FEBRUARY 13, 1848

RIVER CROSSINGS COULD BE VERY DANGEROUS DURING HIGH WATER WHEN ABRAHAM LINCOLN
TRAVELED THE CIRCUIT BY HORSE. HE CROSSED THE MACKINAW RIVER ON THE OLD
EIGHTH JUDICIAL CIRCUIT ROAD AT OR NEAR THIS LOCATION WHILE TRAVELING NORTH TO TREMONT, ILLINOIS.

FOLLOWING THE EIGHTH JUDICIAL CIRCUIT

On yesterday morning the most of the whig members from this District got together and agreed to hold the convention at Tremont in Tazewell county.

LETTER TO JOHN BENNETT, MARCH 7, 1843

THIS GRAVEL ROAD NEAR THE OLD CIRCUIT ROAD ALONG THE MACKINAW RIVER SOUTH OF TREMONT, ILLINOIS,
IS REMINISCENT OF ROADS ABRAHAM LINCOLN REGULARLY TRAVELED, EXCEPT THEY WERE ALL ROUGH, DIRT ROADS.

You remember when I wrote you from Tremont last spring, sending you a little canto of what I called poetry, I promised to bore you with another some time. I now fulfil the promise. LETTER TO ANDREW JOHNSTON, SEPTEMBER 6, 1846

Perhaps you have forgotten me. Dont you remember a long black fellow who rode on horseback with you from Tremont to Springfield nearly ten years ago, swiming your horses over the Mackinaw on the trip? Well, I am that same one fellow yet. LETTER TO JOSEPHUS HEWETT, FEBRUARY 13, 1848

One Sunday in April 1850, Lincoln received an invitation to dine at this house, known as the "Red Brick." Embarrassed by his shabby attire, he protested: "I am ragged! I cannot meet the ladies with my elbows out." But he was eventually prevailed upon to accept. Eugenia Jones recalled that he wore a black alpaca coat and "was seedy, as the lawyers were frequently away from their homes five and six weeks, chiefly owing to the wretched roads and unreliable transportation." One of the ladies attending the supper at the Jones's home whispered to Mrs. Jones, "just look at Mr. Lincoln with his elbows out." As he bade his hostess good bye, Lincoln "apologized for his shabby coat, saying: 'you know, Mrs. Jones, that traveling is very laborious.'" On another occasion, while dining at the Red Brick, Lincoln noticed that one of the Jones children was limping. "Sonny, come here," Lincoln said. He inspected the lad's foot, which had a stone bruise, then pulled out a penknife, opened the bruise, pocketed his knife, and "resumed his supper and humorous conversation."

ABRAHAM LINCOLN STAYED IN TREMONT AT THE HOME OF AN ASSOCIATE, JOHN A. JONES, WHILE TRAVELING THE CIRCUIT. JONES'S DAUGHTER EUGENIA WROTE A BOOK OF RECOLLECTIONS ABOUT LINCOLN'S VISITS TO THE HOME.

... I am annoyed at not being able to remember the christian name of your son who formerly resided at Metamora in Woodford county. I esteem him as one of my best friends; and you will oblige me by handing him this letter, and telling him to write me at once about any thing he pleases, so that I can get his name right.

Letter to Ignatius R. Simms, March 4, 1848

In 1899, Judge David McCulloch recalled seeing Lincoln at the Metamora Courthouse: "David Davis, clad in a gray and apparently homespun suit, with heavy-soled boots on his feet, one leg thrown over the low desk in front of him, his steel gray hair cropped short was presiding. Mr. Lincoln sat among the lawyers with his chair thrown back and his hands clasped behind his head. I was struck with the largeness of all his features especially his ears, which seemed out of all proportion."

At Metamora in 1857, Lincoln represented Melissa Goings, an elderly woman accused of murdering her husband. She claimed that she had acted in self-defense. During a recess in the trial, she fled Illinois, eventually winding up on the Pacific coast. When the court bailiff said that Lincoln had suggested she flee, he allegedly replied: "I didn't run her off. She wanted to know where she could get a good drink of water, and I told her there was mighty good water in Tennessee." She evidently settled in California, where she lived undisturbed by the Illinois authorities for the remainder of her life. In 2009, a statue of Lincoln and Melissa Goings was erected across the street from the courthouse.

An office on the second floor of the Metamora Courthouse State Historic Site.

The Metamora Courthouse is one of only two remaining original courthouses in their original locations from the Eighth Judicial Circuit where Abraham Lincoln practiced law, Metamora Courthouse State Historic Site, Metamora, Illinois.

When we reached Springfield, I staid but one day when I started on this tedious circuit where I now am.   LETTER TO MARY SPEED FROM BLOOMINGTON, FEBRUARY 13, 1848

ABOVE: PANTHER CREEK FORD IS AN OLD STREAM CROSSING NORTH OF CONGERVILLE, ILLINOIS. ABRAHAM LINCOLN FREQUENTLY TRAVELED THROUGH FORDS AND MIGHT HAVE USED THIS FORD WHEN TRAVELING NEAR THE MACKINAW RIVER BETWEEN METAMORA AND BLOOMINGTON.

FOLLOWING PAGE: ABRAHAM LINCOLN CROSSED THE MACKINAW RIVER AT LEAST TWICE ON EACH TRIP FOLLOWING THE CIRCUIT.

... I know how painful it must be to an honest, sincere man, to be urged by his party to the support of a measure, which on his conscience he believes to be wrong. You have had a severe struggle with yourself, and you have determined not to swallow the wrong.

LETTER TO JOHN M. PALMER, SEPTEMBER 7, 1854

Lincoln's good friend and fellow attorney Leonard Swett recalled that on the circuit the "roads were simply trails," the streams were "without bridges, and often swollen and had to be swum," the "sloughs often muddy and almost impassable, and we had to help the horses when the wagon mired down with fence-rails for pries." Once when the caravan of lawyers and judges approached a shallow creek, Lincoln puckishly warned that it was deep and advised his colleagues to strip off their clothes and ride their horses across it. Shivering in the cold air, they complied and rode into the water, which barely reached their mounts' fetlocks. Lincoln enjoyed his prank hugely and remarked, "I don't think a bridge across the stream would interfere with navigation!"

Judge David Davis, who presided over the eighth circuit from 1848 to 1862, wrote numerous letters describing vividly that peripatetic existence. He complained that "traveling in Illinois, and being eaten up by bed bugs and mosquitoes . . . is not what it is cracked up to be." One day in 1852, he told his wife how he and his companions waited for a ferry to convey them across the Sangamon River: "Could not cross. For 2 hours staid in rain, waiting for Ferryman. Swam the horses, took the buggy over straddle a canoe." Davis informed his brother-in-law that "Bad roads, broken bridges, swimming of horses, and constant wetting, are the main incidents in western travel." Especially bothersome were the slews, "miniature swamps, miry and sticky, and extremely difficult to cross with teams and wagons."

Fellow-citizens of Bloomington and McLean County: I am glad to meet you after a longer separation than has been common between you and me. I thank you for the good report you made of the election in Old McLean. REMARKS ON NOVEMBER 21, 1860

THE BRICK PORTION OF THE MILLER-DAVIS BUILDING IS THE OLDEST COMMERCIAL BUILDING IN BLOOMINGTON, ILLINOIS.
THE SMALLER WHITE WOODEN BUILDING ON THE RIGHT IS A REPRODUCTION OF THE DAVID DAVIS LAW OFFICE.
MAJOR'S HALL, THE BUILDING WHERE LINCOLN DELIVERED THE "LOST SPEECH" ON MAY 29, 1856,
WAS LOCATED ACROSS FRONT STREET, DIRECTLY TO THE SOUTH OF THE MILLER-DAVIS BUILDING.

As yet, the wind is an untamed, and unharnessed force; and quite possibly one of the greatest discoveries hereafter to be made, will be the taming, and harnessing of the wind.

First lecture on "Discoveries and Inventions", presented to Young Men's Association of Bloomington, April 6, 1858

In May 1856, the Illinois Republican party was born at a convention held in Bloomington. There Lincoln gave the keynote speech, which auditors alleged was one of his greatest oratorical efforts. Unfortunately, no full account of it appeared in the press, and it has therefore become known as the "Lost Speech." A delegate to the convention described its delivery and reception: "For an hour and a half he held the assemblage spell-bound by the power of his argument, the intense irony of his invective, and the deep earnestness and fervid brilliancy of his eloquence. When he concluded, the audience sprang to their feet, and cheer after cheer told how deeply their hearts had been touched, and their souls warmed up to a generous enthusiasm." The Bloomington Pantagraph said of it: "Several most heart-stirring and powerful speeches were made during the Convention; but without being invidious, we must say that Mr. Lincoln, on Thursday evening, surpassed all others – even himself. His points were unanswerable, and the force and power of his appeals, irresistible."

Lincoln made good friends on the circuit, most notably Judge David Davis, who "loved and admired Lincoln." A prominent Illinois Republican, Gustave Koerner, recalled that Lincoln was "more intimate with him [Davis] than with any other man." Lincoln, in Koerner's opinion, was "kind, just, and, very often, too indulgent to his friends, but those persons for whom he really entertained strong feelings of friendship could be counted on the fingers of one hand. Judge Davis, however, to my certain knowledge was one of them." Their friendship flourished even though few men differed more in their appearance and temperament. Davis had a "positive, decisive character" while Lincoln's was "suave and more yielding." Lincoln was indifferent to money and lived modestly; Davis was a shrewd investor who became rich. Lincoln's sartorial insouciance was legendary; Davis was something of a Beau Brummel. Davis was five inches shorter and a hundred pounds heavier than Lincoln. The judge had attended college and law school; Lincoln had spent less than twelve months in frontier blab schools.

ABRAHAM LINCOLN VISITED HIS ASSOCIATE REUBEN BENJAMIN AT HIS HOME IN BLOOMINGTON WHILE TRAVELING THE CIRCUIT.

FOLLOWING THE EIGHTH JUDICIAL CIRCUIT

You have with you my good friend Judge David Davis; and allow [me] to assure you, you were never associated with a better man. Please present him my respects. Yours very truly A. Lincoln LETTER TO JOSEPH HOLT, NOVEMBER 12, 1861

David Davis and Lincoln did share some things in common: they were devoted to the Whig party; each had "an integrity of character that was immovable in its steadfastness;" they both "were princes of geniality and capital story-tellers." Judge John M. Scott believed that the two "were greater because of their close association and had the benefit of each others peculiar qualities." Lincoln "planned and looked far into the future to discover what the end of a proposed measure would be," while "Davis with his abrupt energy and impulsive purpose to overcome all opposition, carried into effect much of what Lincoln devised." Neither of them "would ever have occupied the exalted positions they did, had it not been for the helpful influence each exerted for the other. Lincoln knew Davis' great powers and that a close alliance with him was necessary to him in developing his own plans and purposes." Davis possessed "much ability to organize political forces and nothing afforded more gratification than to exercise his powers in that direction on behalf of Mr. Lincoln in whom he then saw or thought he saw evidences of his coming greatness." Whereas "Lincoln knew better what ought to be done in political matters," Davis "knew better how to do it." Lincoln, "always quiet and most deliberate in all he said and did concerning grave political questions," contrasted sharply with Davis, who "was vehemently impulsive, forceful and resolute in effort to accomplish that which was planned for him to do or in whatever he purposed himself to do."

ABOVE AND FOLLOWING PAGE: THE BARN AND STABLE AT THE DAVID DAVIS MANSION STATE HISTORIC SITE ARE PART OF THE ORIGINAL HOMESTEAD WHERE ABRAHAM LINCOLN WAS OFTEN A GUEST. LINCOLN LIKELY STABLED HIS HORSE HERE WHEN HE STAYED WITH DAVID DAVIS WHILE IN BLOOMINGTON, ILLINOIS. (NATIONAL HISTORIC LANDMARK)

FOLLOWING THE EIGHTH JUDICIAL CIRCUIT

The season of the year will be most favorable for good roads and pleasant weather; and although we cannot but believe you would be highly gratified with such a visit to the prairie-land, the pleasure it would give us, and thousands such as we, is beyond all question.

LETTER TO HENRY CLAY, AUGUST 29, 1842

WHAT ONCE WAS AN EVERYDAY SIGHT TO ABRAHAM LINCOLN WHILE TRAVELING PRAIRIE ROADS, HAS DISAPPEARED. A LANE PASSES THROUGH THE AUTUMN WILDFLOWERS AND PRAIRIE GRASSES AT SUGAR GROVE PRAIRIE NORTHEAST OF MCLEAN, ILLINOIS, NEAR THE LOCATION OF THE OLD CIRCUIT ROAD LINCOLN TRAVELED BETWEEN BLOOMINGTON AND LOGAN COUNTY.

Circuit-riding lawyers, usually covered with either mud or dust when they arrived at a county seat, were immediately set upon by would-be clients who, according to Lincoln's partner William H. Herndon, were "eagerly seeking to engage their favorite counsel. No sooner had the attorneys shed their leggings and overcoats than potential clients began offering short accounts of their cases." All "was bustle and excitement" as pleas and answers were prepared, demurrers filed, bills in chancery drawn, and preparations for trial made. All "this heterogeneous mass of business was rushed in upon them in a manner which would have confused any mind not well trained to that mode of practicing law." Often lawyers were enlisted "to take part in a trial when the jury was already being called, and they must learn the case during the trial itself." This system "compelled everybody to think quickly and to act promptly."

At noon on Monday the court usually convened. The early afternoon was consumed in summoning and swearing in the grand and petit jurors and having the grand jury consider indictments. (In election years, the afternoon and evening of the first court day would be devoted to political speeches by the attorneys.) The sheriff chose jurors, who were often the same men from one term to the next, "personal friends of Judge Davis, men of intelligence, sound judgment and integrity whose verdicts rarely had to be set aside." Cases in default, where one party failed to appear, were quickly disposed of, and testimony was taken in ex parte cases, like uncontested divorces. Around 4 p.m. the court adjourned, to reassemble Tuesday morning at 8 a.m. For the rest of the day, Herndon recalled, "we lawyers would take a ramble in the woods – over the prairies – or through the village – anywhere to kill time – take a [card] game of 'old sledge' or euchre . . . – in short anything to while away time. On such tramps we would discuss politics – talk over our cases." Egalitarianism prevailed among the townspeople and the sociable lawyers, who put on no airs.

LEFT: PRAIRIE GRASSES SILHOUETTED IN THE EVENING TWILIGHT.   RIGHT: A FULL MOON RISES OVER THE PRAIRIE.

Following the Eighth Judicial Circuit

As to my personal movements this summer, and fall, I am quite busy trying to pick up my lost crumbs of last year. I shall be here till September; then to the circuit till the 20th. then to Cincinnati, awhile, after a Patent right case; and back to the circuit to the end of November. I can be seen here any time this month; and at Bloomington at any time from the 10th. to the 17th. of September.

LETTER TO OWEN LOVEJOY, AUGUST 11, 1855

OX-EYE SUNFLOWER IN FULL BLOOM ON A FOGGY SUMMER MORNING AT SUGAR GROVE PRAIRIE NEAR MCLEAN, ILLINOIS.

If I cannot rightfully murder a man, I may tie him to the tail of a kicking horse, and let him kick the man to death. SPEECH AT BLOOMINGTON, APRIL 10, 1860

Circuit court proceedings were often "meager and uninteresting." The Danville Vermilion County Press complained that the circuit court was "always encumbered and overcrowded" with minor cases involving liquor law violations. Their "wearying, troublesome littleness drags out the time of the court, and prevents application to cases of more importance." In the early years of the circuit, cases usually involved assault and battery, suits on promissory notes, minor disputes, slander, horse trading, petty larceny. Now and then a murder or manslaughter case was tried. In the 1830s and 1840s, the population of Illinois was small, society primitive, land plentiful, employment easy to find, and litigation quite simple. Cases originating in debt often generated other actions. As Milton Hay, a friend of Lincoln, recalled "if a man had an uncollectable debt, the current phrase was 'I'll take it out of his hide.' This would bring on an action for assault and battery. The free comments of the neighbors on the fracas, or the character of the parties, would be productive of slander suits." Similarly, a "man would for his convenience lay down an irascible neighbor's fence and indolently forget to put it up again – and an action of trespass would grow out of it. The suit would lead to a free fight and sometimes furnish the bloody incidents for a murder trial." Henry C. Whitney thought it "strange to contemplate that in those . . . primitive days, Mr. Lincoln's whole attention should have been engrossed in petty controversies or acrimonious disputes between neighbors about trifles; that he should have puzzled his great mind in attempting to decipher who was the owner of a litter of pigs, or which party was to blame for the loss of a flock of sheep, by foot rot; or whether some irascible spirit was justified in avowing that his enemy had committed perjury; yet I have known him to give as earnest attention to such matters, as, later, he gave to affairs of state."

BLACK-EYED SUSANS IN PEAK BLOOM AT SUGAR GROVE PRAIRIE NEAR THE OLD CIRCUIT ROAD.

FOLLOWING THE EIGHTH JUDICIAL CIRCUIT

We were thunderstruck . . . When the storm shall be past, he shall find us still Americans; no less devoted to the continued Union and prosperity of the country than heretofore.

SPEECH AT PEORIA, OCTOBER 16, 1854

ABOVE: THUNDERSTORMS AND LIGHTNING WERE HAZARDS LINCOLN FACED WHILE
TRAVELING THE OPEN COUNTRY THROUGH ILLINOIS, SUGAR GROVE PRAIRIE.

FOLLOWING LEFT: PASSING OF THE STORM AS COMPASS PLANTS SWAY IN THE WIND.
FOLLOWING RIGHT: PRAIRIE GRASSES SWAY IN STRONG WIND AS A STORM PASSES SUGAR GROVE PRAIRIE.

In the course of my main argument, Judge Douglas interrupted me to say, that the principle of the Nebraska bill was very old; that it originated when God made man and placed good and evil before him, allowing him to choose for himself, being responsible for the choice he should make. At the time I thought this was merely playful; and I answered it accordingly. But in his reply to me he renewed it, as a serious argument. In seriousness then, the facts of this proposition are not true as stated. God did not place good and evil before man, telling him to make his choice. On the contrary, he did tell him there was one tree, of the fruit of which, he should not eat, upon pain of certain death. I should scarcely wish so strong a prohibition against slavery in Nebraska.

SPEECH AT PEORIA, OCTOBER 16, 1854

Lincoln did not complain much about life on the circuit because he loved it. In explaining why he turned down an offer to become a partner with a Chicago attorney, Lincoln (according to Judge David Davis) "gave as a reason that he tended to Consumption – That if he went to Chicago that he would have to sit down and Study hard – That it would Kill him – That he would rather go around the Circuit . . . than to sit down & die in Chicago. In my opinion I think Mr Lincoln was happy – as happy as he could be, when on this Circuit – and happy no other place. This was his place of Enjoyment. As a general rule when all the lawyers of a Saturday Evening would go home and see their families & friends at home Lincoln would refuse to go home." Just as Lincoln was unique in avoiding home on weekends, he was one of the very few who traveled the entire circuit each spring and fall. Most attorneys stayed close to home, attending only those circuit courts in counties adjacent to their own. Even after railroads connecting Springfield with most of the county seats were completed in the mid-1850s, Lincoln seldom returned home on weekends.

Following the Eighth Judicial Circuit

The matter now takes me at great disadvantage, in this, that it will cost me more to leave the Circuit (which has just commenced) and attend to taking proof, than it would to give up the claim; and your letter does not mention the time of your next term.

LETTER TO GEORGE B. KINKEAD, SEPTEMBER 13, 1853

ABOVE: INDIAN GRASS AND LITTLE BLUESTEM ON A CALM AUTUMN EVENING AT SUGAR GROVE PRAIRIE NEAR MCLEAN, ILLINOIS.

FOLLOWING PAGE: THE SUN SETS OVER A CALM PRAIRIE AT SUGAR GROVE PRAIRIE.

Lincoln charged notoriously low fees. After successfully representing a client in a complicated slander suit, Lincoln asked for $25. "We were astonished," recalled opposing counsel, "and had he said one hundred dollars it would have been what we expected. The judgment [$600] was a large one for those days: he had attended the case at two terms of court, had been engaged for two days in a hotly-contested suit, and his client's adversary was going to pay the bill. The simplicity of Mr. Lincoln's character in money matters is well illustrated by the fact that for all this he charged twenty-five dollars." In 1856, he wrote a client saying: "I have just received yours of the 16th, with check on Flagg & Savage for twenty-five dollars. You must think I am a high-priced man. You are too liberal with your money. Fifteen dollars is enough for the job. I send you a receipt for fifteen dollars, and return to you a ten-dollar bill." When Lincoln charged the Chicago banking firm of George Smith and Company a mere $25 for trying and winning their case, the head of the firm thanked John W. Bunn for recommending Lincoln, saying: "We asked you to get the best lawyer in Springfield and it certainly looks as if you had secured one of the cheapest." After offering advice to a young man about collecting a debt, Lincoln refused to accept any money for the consultation. When the client insisted "that he should be allowed to make some present" as compensation, Lincoln replied: "when you go down stairs just stop at the stationers, and send me up a bottle of ink." For collecting $2000 for a client who had lent that sum to a deadbeat, Lincoln charged a fee of only $2.

In notes for a law lecture, Lincoln stressed that the "matter of fees is important, far beyond the mere question of bread and butter involved. Properly attended to, fuller justice is done to both lawyer and client. An exorbitant fee should never be claimed. As a general rule never take your whole fee in advance, nor any more than a small retainer. When fully paid beforehand, you are more than a common mortal if you can feel the same interest in the case as if something were still in prospect for you, as well as for your client. And when you lack interest in the case the job will very likely lack skill and diligence in the performance. Settle the amount of fee and take a note in advance. Then you will feel that you are working for something, and you are sure to do your work faithfully and well. Never sell a fee note — at least not before the consideration service is performed. It leads to negligence by losing interest in the case, and dishonesty in refusing to refund when you have allowed the consideration to fail."

What points, in our Rail Road cases, were decided at the Spring term of your Circuit Court?

ABOVE: A NATIVE SUNFLOWER BLOOMS IN EARLY AUTUMN FOLLOWING HEAVY RAIN AT SUGAR GROVE PRAIRIE, NEAR McLEAN, ILLINOIS.

FOLLOWING PAGE: COMPASS PLANTS GROW IN A REMNANT OF NATIVE PRAIRIE ALONG RAILROAD TRACKS NEAR ATLANTA, ILLINOIS. THIS SCENE WAS COMMON IN THE 1850s WHEN RAILROADS BEGAN CROSSING THE PRAIRIES.

Dear Sir

I have to day drawn on you in favor of the McLean County Bank, or rather it's cashier, for one hundred and fifty dollars. This is intended as a fee for all services done by me for the Illinois Central Railroad, since last September, within the counties of McLean and De Witt. Within that term, and in the two counties, I have assisted, for the Road, in at least fifteen cases (I believe, one or two more) and I have concluded to lump them off at ten dollars a case. With this explanation, I shall be obliged if you will honor the draft.

Yours truly A. Lincoln

LETTER TO JAMES F. JOY, SEPTEMBER 14, 1855

During the late 1840s and the 1850s, a new chapter in the history of Illinois opened. In 1848, the adoption of a new state constitution, the completion of the Illinois and Michigan Canal, the launching of a rail line connecting Chicago with Galena, and the arrival of a presidential message via the telegraph for the first time – all combined to herald the end of the frontier era. Hastening social and economic change were the rapid expansion of the rail network (from 111 miles in 1850 to 2,790 in 1860) and the doubling of the population (from 851,470 in 1850 to 1,711,951 in 1860). Railroads slashed travel time between Springfield and Chicago from three days to twelve hours. The 705-mile Illinois Central Railroad system, begun in 1851, was the world's longest when completed five years later. Because lawyers found more and more business in their own towns, they no longer spent weeks and months traveling from one county seat to another in quest of clients. By the end of the decade, only Lincoln and a couple of others continued attending court throughout the circuit.

Following the Eighth Judicial Circuit

This change, I suppose, will be agreeable to you, as it will give you larger audiences, and much easier travel—nearly all being by railroad. LETTER TO CASSIUS CLAY, AUGUST 10, 1860

Lawyers on the circuit practiced at county seats. Upon arriving at one, Lincoln and his colleagues would scarcely have time to dismount before local residents accosted them. For the inhabitants of the county seats, trials provided both entertainment and enlightenment. "The courthouse was the center of interest for the mass of people who were generally uncultured and ignorant," William Herndon recounted. "When court commenced people flocked to the county seat to see and to hear and to learn. Eloquence was in demand," for "the people loved to hear talk – talk." The attorneys realized this and it "made them ambitious to succeed and conquer." Most of them were "young and ambitious, struggling each in his way to acquire glory. If a young lawyer made a fine speech and tickled the crowd – was eloquent and gained his case he got the hearty applause of the people & glory too. His fame was fixed at once." Frontiersmen in the 1830s and 1840s "had no newspapers to tell them daily the history of the world, and hence did not read much but kept their ears & eyes open. Men flocked to the courthouse to hear men talk during court hours & to hear jokes & stories of a night." The "courthouse supplied the place of theatres, lecture and concert rooms, and other places of interest and amusement." There "leading lawyers and judges were the star actors, and had each his partisans." Thus, "crowds attended the courts to see the judges, to hear the lawyers contend with argument, and law, and wit for success, victory and fame." To the country folk, the assembling of the court was a welcome break in the monotony of rural life. "The semi-annual shopping of the country districts was transacted during court week: the wits and county statesmen contributed their stock of pleasantry and philosophy; the local belles came in to see and be seen: and the courthouse, from 'early morn to dewy eve,' and the tavern from dewy eve to early morn, were replete with bustle, business, energy, hilarity, novelty, irony, sarcasm, excitement and eloquence."

CATTAILS SILHOUETTED AT SUNSET ON A POND SOUTH OF BLOOMINGTON NEAR THE OLD EIGHTH JUDICIAL CIRCUIT ROAD.
IN LINCOLN'S TIME, WETLANDS AND MARSHES WERE A COMMON SIGHT.

FOLLOWING THE EIGHTH JUDICIAL CIRCUIT

Gentlemen

Your despach, requesting me to deliver a speech at Bloomington is received. I very much prefer to make no more speeches soon; but if, as friends of mine, you can not excuse me, it is not much odds when—say, the evening of Tuesday the 10th. Inst.

Yours as ever A. Lincoln

LETTER TO WILLIAM C. HOBBS AND WILLIAM H. HANNA, APRIL 6, 1860

THIS LANE RUNS PAST AN OLD COUNTRY CEMETERY NEAR THE LOCATION OF THE HOBLIT HALF-WAY HOUSE AND THE OLD CIRCUIT ROAD, SOUTHEAST OF ATLANTA, ILLINOIS, WHERE ABRAHAM LINCOLN WOULD STAY THE NIGHT WHILE TRAVELING THE CIRCUIT.

There is a vague popular belief that lawyers are necessarily dishonest. I say vague, because when we consider to what extent confidence and honors are reposed in and conferred upon lawyers by the people, it appears improbable that their impression of dishonesty is very distinct and vivid. Yet the impression is common, almost universal. Let no young man choosing the law for a calling for a moment yield to the popular belief—resolve to be honest at all events; and if in your own judgment you cannot be an honest lawyer, resolve to be honest without being a lawyer. Choose some other occupation, rather than one in the choosing of which you do, in advance, consent to be a knave.

NOTES FOR A LAW LECTURE, YEAR UNCERTAIN

While on the circuit, Lincoln allegedly lodged often at the Half-Way House, located midway between Bloomington and the town of Lincoln (formerly known as Postville) in Logan County. Samuel Hoblit of Ohio operated that two-story frame hostelry. Once when Lincoln arrived there he found no one home except the host's adolescent son John, who fixed a meal for his guest. That began a long-term friendship. When John left his parents' home, he established residence just outside the village of Atlanta. There Lincoln would stay on occasion. In 1858, Lincoln reportedly called only to discover that John's home had burned down and that his family were reduced to living in a nearby shed. Though they offered to obtain better accommodations for Lincoln, he insisted on staying with them in the shed. Soon thereafter John's wife delivered a son, who was christened Abraham Lincoln Hoblit.

ABRAHAM LINCOLN SPENT THE NIGHT IN THIS SHED SOUTHEAST OF ATLANTA, ILLINOIS,
AT THE INVITATION OF THE JOHN HOBLIT FAMILY AFTER THEY HAD BEEN DISPLACED FROM THEIR HOME BY A FIRE.

I am passing on my way to Chicago, and am happy in doing so to be able to meet so many of my friends in Logan County, and if to do no more, to exchange with you the compliments of the season, and to thank you for the many kindnesses you have manifested toward me.   REMARKS AT LINCOLN, ILLINOIS, NOVEMBER 21, 1860

The preacher, it is said, advocates temperance because he is a fanatic, and desires a union of Church and State; the lawyer, from his pride and vanity of hearing himself speak; and the hired agent, for his salary.   TEMPERANCE ADDRESS, FEBRUARY 22, 1842

Built in 1840, this structure served as a courthouse only until 1848, when the Logan County seat was transferred from Postville to Mount Pulaski. In 1929, Henry Ford moved the building to Dearborn, Michigan, where (in a remodeled configuration) it can be seen at Greenfield Village, part of the Henry Ford Museum complex. The replica in Lincoln (Postville was renamed Lincoln in 1853) was constructed in 1953 as part of the town's centennial celebration. In addition to the courtroom, the structure housed a tavern as well as an office used by the county clerk, sheriff, recorder of deeds, coroner, and surveyor.

The town of Lincoln, Illinois, the only municipality named for Lincoln during his lifetime, was founded in 1853 to accommodate the Illinois Central Railroad, which needed a passenger-depot-cum-water-stop between Bloomington and Springfield. The enterprising men who bought the land for the town site hired Lincoln to handle the necessary paperwork. The town's founders decided to name it after their attorney. A teetotaler of long standing, Lincoln then christened the new city, using the juice of a watermelon instead of the more traditional champagne.

ABOVE: THIS REPLICA OF THE POSTVILLE COURTHOUSE WHERE LINCOLN PRACTICED LAW IS
ON THE ORIGINAL LOCATION, POSTVILLE COURTHOUSE STATE HISTORIC SITE, LINCOLN, ILLINOIS.

PREVIOUS PAGE: THE COURTROOM OF THE POSTVILLE COURTHOUSE STATE HISTORIC SITE, THE ORIGINAL SEAT OF LOGAN COUNTY.

Following the Eighth Judicial Circuit

By this mail I send you a specimen copy of the new german paper started here. I think you could not do a more efficient service than to get it a few subscribers, if possible. I have sent a copy to Capps at Pulaski.

Yours as ever A. Lincoln LETTER TO FREDERICK C.W. KOEHNLE, JULY 11, 1859

ABOVE: THE MOUNT PULASKI COURTHOUSE IS ONE OF ONLY TWO REMAINING ORIGINAL COURTHOUSES IN THEIR ORIGINAL LOCATIONS FROM THE EIGHTH JUDICIAL CIRCUIT WHERE ABRAHAM LINCOLN PRACTICED LAW, MOUNT PULASKI COURTHOUSE STATE HISTORIC SITE, MOUNT PULASKI, ILLINOIS.

FOLLOWING PAGE: THE JURY SECTION IN THE SECOND FLOOR COURTROOM OF THE MOUNT PULASKI COURTHOUSE STATE HISTORIC SITE.

The enclosed letters I wrote last night, but when I went to the Post-office this morning your mail had left about half an hour. So I send them by Mr. Harris. Will you please take out the one addressed to you, and drop the others in your Post-office, unless you see the men to hand them to in person, in which case please do that.

LETTER TO JOHN BENNETT, JANUARY 16, 1846

I am ashamed of not sooner answering your letter, herewith returned; and, my only appologies are, first, that I have been very busy in the U.S. court; and second, that when I received the letter I put it in my old hat, and buying a new one the next day, the old one was set aside, and so, the letter lost sight of for a time.

LETTER TO RICHARD THOMAS, JUNE 27, 1850

The Mount Pulaski Courthouse was built in 1848 and served as Logan County's government headquarters until 1855, when the county seat moved to the town of Lincoln (formerly Postville). Here in 1853 Lincoln participated in a patent suit known as "the horological cradle" case. It involved a contraption which was to be "rocked by machinery with a weight running on one or more pulleys; the cradle constituting the pendulum and which, being wound up, would rock itself, thus saving the continual labor to mother and nurses of rocking the cradle." Lincoln's partner, William H. Herndon, recalled the case: "Although Lincoln and I were duly retained, Mr. Lincoln, owing to his natural bent for the study of mechanical appliances, soon became so enamoured of the case that he assumed entire charge of our end of it. The model of the machine was for a time exhibited in a store window in town and eventually reached our office where Mr. Lincoln became deeply absorbed in it. He would dilate at great length on its merits for the benefit of our callers or any one else who happened into the office and manifested the least interest in it." When the judge asked how the cradle could be stopped, Lincoln quipped: "The thing's like some of the glib and interesting talkers you and I know; when it gets to going it doesn't know when to stop."

Following the Eighth Judicial Circuit

Ten days afterwards, I met the Judge at Clinton—that is to say, I was on the ground, but not in the discussion—and heard him make a speech.... When the Judge spoke at Clinton, he came very near making a charge of falsehood against me.

First Lincoln-Douglas Debate, August 21, 1858

Abraham Lincoln often partnered with Clifton H. Moore when practicing law in Clinton, Illinois. Lincoln worked on law cases in the C.H. Moore Law Office next to the town square while traveling the Eighth Judicial Circuit.

... I only ask my friends and all who are eager for the truth, that when they hear me represented as saying or meaning anything strange, they will turn to my own words and examine for themselves. I do not wish Douglas to put words into my mouth. I do not wish him to construe my words as he pleases, and then represent me as meaning what he wishes me to mean, but I do wish the people to read and judge for themselves.

SPEECH AT CLINTON, JULY 27, 1858

Ohio-born Clifton H. Moore (1817-1901) moved to Pekin, Illinois in 1839, where he served as a schoolteacher briefly. After reading law in a local firm, he gained admission to the bar in 1841 and promptly moved to Clinton, where he practiced law and engaged in business. In 1852, Clifton H. Moore and David Davis established a real estate partnership and made a great deal of money speculating in land. Lincoln and Moore were co-counsel forty-nine times and opposed each other in thirty-six cases. Like Lincoln, Moore was a Whig and later became a Republican. Unlike Lincoln, he did not aspire to hold public office.

Lincoln and Moore worked on so many railroad cases that they formed what was virtually a seasonal partnership. Sometimes they represented opposite sides at the Clinton Courthouse. In 1855, one William Dungey alleged that a certain Joseph Spencer had wrongfully accused him of being a black man. In presenting Dungey's case to the jury, Lincoln was, as one of the opposing counsel recalled, "both entertaining and effective. A dramatic and powerful stroke was his direct reference to Spencer's accusation that Dungey was a 'nigger.' I hear him now as he said: 'Gentlemen of the jury, my client is not a Negro, though it is no crime to be a Negro. His skin may not be as white as ours, but I say he is not a Negro, though he may be a Moor.'" Moore served on Spencer's defense team.

Moore and Lincoln were such good friends that when Lincoln was entitled to choose a parcel of government land as a reward for his service in the Black Hawk War, he took Moore's advice and selected a tract in Iowa near property owned by Moore, who acted as his representative and paid his real estate taxes.

BUILT IN 1856, THE C.H. MOORE LAW OFFICE APPEARS MUCH THE SAME
AS IT DID WHEN ABRAHAM LINCOLN WORKED IN THE OFFICE.

Mr. C. H. Moore, of De Witt county, sends you a record asking an order for a supersedeas. If you allow it, Mr. Moore himself is abundantly good for surety, and we desire that you name him as such in the order.

Very truly Your friend A. Lincoln

LETTER TO JOHN D. CATON, MARCH 21, 1856

For two decades Lincoln visited Clinton semi-annually, spending more than a hundred nights there as he practiced law on the circuit. He also made campaign appearances there, including one during the memorable 1858 senatorial contest. On that occasion, Lincoln stayed with Moore and confided his personal view of Stephen A. Douglas's integrity: "Douglas will tell a lie to ten thousand people one day, even though he knows he may have to deny it to five thousand the next."

When Lincoln died, Moore delivered a eulogy at Clinton, concluding with these moving words: "In him, next to God we trusted. Trusted in his honesty, that was never tarnished; trusted in his mercy, that was only equaled by Him who said 'Father forgive them for they know not what they do.' Above all, we trusted him because he had power and had not abused it."

ABOVE: ABRAHAM LINCOLN STAYED AS A GUEST AT THE HOME OF CLIFTON H. MOORE IN CLINTON, ILLINOIS,
WHILE FOLLOWING THE EIGHTH JUDICIAL CIRCUIT.

PREVIOUS PAGE: SUNRISE ON THE C.H. MOORE LAW OFFICE IN CLINTON, ONE BLOCK FROM THE SITE OF THE
ORIGINAL DEWITT COUNTY COURTHOUSE. CLINTON WAS ONE OF THE TOWNS ON THE EIGHTH JUDICIAL CIRCUIT
WHERE ABRAHAM LINCOLN PRACTICED LAW FOR ALMOST TWENTY YEARS.

FOLLOWING THE EIGHTH JUDICIAL CIRCUIT

It pains me to have to say that I forgot to attend to your business when I was in Clinton, at court in May last. Your best way would be to address me a letter at Clinton, about the time I go there to court in the fall (Oct. 16th. I think) and then it will be fresh, & I will not forget or neglect it.   Yours truly A. Lincoln

LETTER TO MILTON K. ALEXANDER, JUNE 13, 1854

AN OLD WHITE OAK TREE STANDS ON THE NORTHERN SIDE OF WELDON SPRINGS STATE PARK, EAST OF CLINTON, ILLINOIS, NEAR THE LOCATION OF THE OLD CIRCUIT ROAD.

At the hazard of wearing this point thread bare, I will relate an anecdote, which seems too strikingly in point to be omitted.

SPEECH ON THE SUB-TREASURY, DECEMBER [26], 1839

Lincoln's legendary talent as a storyteller helped him win over juries. "Not infrequently Mr. Lincoln would illustrate his legal arguments with an appropriate story or anecdote," Judge John M. Scott recalled. "That line of legal argument with many lawyers would be a most dangerous experiment but it never failed with Mr. Lincoln. When he chose to do so he could place the opposite party and his counsel too for that matter in a most ridiculous attitude by relating in his inimitable way a pertinent story. That often gave him a great advantage with the jury." Scott cited the example of a young attorney who "had brought an action in trespass to recover damages done to his client's growing crops by defendant's hogs. The right of action under the law of Illinois as it was then depended on . . . whether the plaintiff's fence was sufficient to turn ordinary stock. There was some little conflict in the evidence on that question but the weight of the testimony was decidedly in favor of plaintiff and sustained beyond all doubt his cause of action. Mr. Lincoln appeared for a defendant. There was no controversy as to the damage by defendant's stock. The only thing in the case that could possibly admit of any discussion was the condition of plaintiff's fence and as the testimony on that question seemed to be in favor of plaintiff and as the sum involved was little in amount, Mr. Lincoln did not deem it necessary to argue the case seriously but by way of saying something in behalf of his client he told a little story about a fence that was so crooked that when a hog went through an opening in it, invariably it came out on the same side from whence it started."

[Continued on page 133]

LEFT: AN OLD WHITE OAK STANDS NEAR THE OAK ON THE PREVIOUS PAGE AT WELDON SPRINGS.

RIGHT: TWO OLD OAKS SILHOUETTED AT SUNSET AT WELDON SPRINGS STATE PARK.

Following the Eighth Judicial Circuit

At daylight the morning after the election, I had to go to court at De Witt county, and I then had nothing of any account to write you. On my return last night I found your letter.

BLAZING STAR BLOOMS IN A PRAIRIE RESTORATION AT WELDON SPRINGS STATE PARK EAST
OF CLINTON, ILLINOIS, NEAR THE OLD EIGHTH JUDICIAL CIRCUIT ROAD ABRAHAM LINCOLN TRAVELED.

When I was about leaving Washington last I told you an anecdote by way of impressing on your memory the application of Allen Francis to be Consul at Glasgow, Scotland. I very much wish he could be obliged. He is part editor of the oldest paper in the state; and, being a practical printer, has worked constantly, setting type for it, eighteen years. He is tired, and has a right to be. His wife is a "Scotchman" and wishes to visit her father-land.

Your Obt. Servt A. Lincoln

LETTER TO JOHN M. CLAYTON, U.S. SECRETARY OF STATE, AUGUST 12, 1849

"His description of the confused look of the hog after several times going through the fence and still finding itself on the side from where it had started was a humorous specimen of the best story telling. The effect was to make plaintiff's case appear ridiculous and while Mr. Lincoln did not attempt to apply the story to the case, the jury seemed to think it had some kind of application to the fence in controversy – otherwise he would not have told it and shortly returned a verdict for defendant. Few men could have made so much out of so little a story. His manner of telling a story was most generally better than the story itself. He always seemed to have an apt story on hand for use on all occasions. If he had no story in stock he could formulate one instantly so pertinent it would seem he had brought it into service on many previous occasions. It is believed he had never heard before, many of the mirth provoking stories he told at the bar, on the rostrum and elsewhere but formulated them for immediate use. That is a talent akin to the power to construct a parable – a talent that few men possess."

THE SETTING SUN SHINES THROUGH THE INDIAN GRASS IN THE PRAIRIE AT WELDON SPRINGS STATE PARK.

FOLLOWING THE EIGHTH JUDICIAL CIRCUIT

Pardon me for not writing a longer letter. I have a great many letters to write. I was at Monticello Thursday evening. Signs all very good.

Your friend as ever A. Lincoln LETTER TO HENRY C. WHITNEY, AUGUST 2, 1858

BLUEBELLS BLOOMING NEXT TO A LARGE HACKBERRY AND SYCAMORE TREE ALONG THE SANGAMON RIVER, UPSTREAM FROM THE RIVER CROSSING OF THE OLD EIGHTH JUDICIAL CIRCUIT ROAD AT MONTICELLO, ILLINOIS.

In 1859, an Urbana newspaper described the scene when the court was in session: "during the past week, nearly every resident of the county has been in our beautiful city – Courting. The streets have been literally thronged with every imaginable specimen of the genus Homo. Lawyers, judges, clients, honorables, prisoners of all bars, and so forth, besides others, have been in attendance at our Circuit Court. Some think, perhaps, that they have not received justice, while others believe they have a little too much of it. Altogether they have had a lively time." Another Urbana paper lamented that the court dealt with such unimportant matters as "a dog suit, a wood-stealing Irishman, [and] a half-crazy horse thief."

AN OLD STONE WALL AT THE ENTRANCE TO THE BENJAMIN HARRIS HOMESTEAD,
SOUTH OF MAHOMET, ILLINOIS, WHERE ABRAHAM LINCOLN STAYED WHILE TRAVELING THE CIRCUIT.

In the matter of making speeches I am a good [deal] pressed by invitations from almost all quarters; and while I hope to be at Urbana sometime during the canvass I cannot yet say when.

LETTER TO JOSEPH O. CUNNINGHAM, AUGUST 22, 1858

To his Excellency, the Governor of the State of Illinois.

We, the undersigned citizens of Vermilion County respectfully represent that George High was, at the fall term of the Champaign county circuit court, 1855, convicted of the crime of horse-stealing, and sentenced to the penitentiary for the term of three years; that the offence was committed in this county, and the trial was in Champaign by change of venue; that he has now been in the penitentiary more than two years, and was confined in jail about fourteen months previous to his conviction; that most of us took an active interest in procuring his conviction; that we now think public justice has been satisfied in his case; and as he is yet quite a young man, we hope and believe some lenity towards him, would be favorable to his reformation for the future. We therefore respectfully ask that he be pardoned for the remainder of his term.

I have been acquainted with the circumstances of George High's case from the time of his arrest; and I cheerfully join in the request that he may be pardoned.

PETITION TO GOVERNOR WILLIAM H. BISSELL FOR PARDON OF GEORGE HIGH, NOVEMBER 10, 1857

WILD BERGAMOT, YELLOW AND PURPLE CONEFLOWERS, AND COMPASS PLANTS AT MEADOWBROOK PRAIRIE IN URBANA.

A SUMMER THUNDERSTORM APPROACHES MEADOWBROOK PRAIRIE IN URBANA, ILLINOIS,
LOCATED TWO MILES FROM THE OLD URBANA COURTHOUSE SITE WHERE ABRAHAM LINCOLN PRACTICED LAW.

137

Yours of the 14th. is just received. In your case at Danville, I got just so far, and no farther, than to be ready to take testimony for the next term.

LETTER TO WILLIAM H. DAVENPORT, MAY 22, 1858

I am glad I made the late race. It gave me a hearing on the great and durable question of the age, which I could have had in no other way; and though I now sink out of view, and shall be forgotten, I believe I have made some marks which will tell for the cause of civil liberty long after I am gone.

LETTER TO ANSON G. HENRY, NOVEMBER 19, 1858

At Danville in Vermilion County, the extreme eastern end of the circuit, Lincoln teamed up with Ward Hill Lamon, eighteen years his junior, on more than 150 cases. Their quasi-partnership lasted from 1852 to 1857, when the younger man was elected prosecutor of the Seventeenth Judicial Circuit and moved to Bloomington. Lamon was a tall, stout, hard-drinking, humorous, earthy Virginian. Friends described him as "chivalrous, courageous, generous," and "a reckless, dashing, pleasant, social, good looking fellow, an admirable singer, free with money and fond of comic stories," a "brave man" and "a fine boxer" who "was proud of his Herculean frame." No student, he probably never read a book from cover to cover in his entire life. Lamon drummed up business and Lincoln tried the cases. Lincoln "trusted Lamon more than any other man." Lamon's "fascinating manners could not help making him troops of friends." A reporter thought him "the most jolly moral philosopher of the day."

AN OLD PIONEER CEMETERY ON THE LINCOLN TRAIL ROAD NEAR OGDEN, ILLINOIS, DATES TO THE TIME ABRAHAM LINCOLN TRAVELED BY IT ON THE WAY TO DANVILLE.

The Lincoln Trail Road near Ogden, between Champaign-Urbana and Danville, which was part of the old Eighth Judicial Circuit road. Looking east, as powerful June thunderstorms with tornados move through the area.

Following the Eighth Judicial Circuit

When I went to Danville in the fall I found that Don Carlos had not yet been served with process.

LETTER TO WILLIAM H. DAVENPORT, DECEMBER 28, 1857

AN OLD OAK TREE STILL STANDS ALONG THE LINCOLN TRAIL ROAD SOUTH OF MUNCIE, ILLINOIS,
WHERE ABRAHAM LINCOLN TRAVELED THE OLD EIGHTH JUDICIAL CIRCUIT ROAD ON THE WAY TO DANVILLE.

I don't want to be unjustly accused of dealing illiberally or unfairly with an adversary, either in court, or in a political canvass, or anywhere else. I would despise myself if I supposed myself ready to deal less liberally with an adversary than I was willing to be treated myself.

FOURTH LINCOLN DOUGLAS DEBATE AT CHARLESTON, SEPTEMBER 18, 1858

Hiram W. Beckwith, who observed Lincoln practice in Danville, believed that he "had no superior before a jury." Beckwith called Lincoln "an admirable tactician, ready for the surprises and turns of a trial, and quick to change his line of attack or defense as emergency required. He was an adept, both as aggressor and at retort, in the badinage and sparrings of counsel that spice the course of a trial." When necessary, "he gave and took hard blows, though rarely in anger, and apparently enjoyed the rough and tumble contests at nisi prius." Because he was careful not to bore juries, he made few notes during a trial. "Notes are a bother, taking time to make, and more to hunt them up afterward," he told Beckwith. "Lawyers who do so soon get the habit of referring to them so much that it confused and tired the jury." For the same reason, he would not read to jurors from statutes or quote authorities; rather, he would turn to opposing counsel or to the bench and say to the jury, "These gentlemen will allow, or the Judge, if need be, will tell you, that the law of the case is thus or so," and summarize the relevant statute in clear, simple language.

LEFT: THE LINCOLN TRAIL ROAD EAST OF STONY CREEK NEAR MUNCIE.

RIGHT: A LARGE COTTONWOOD TREE ON THE BLUFF WEST OF STONY CREEK ALONG THE LINCOLN TRAIL ROAD.

FOLLOWING THE EIGHTH JUDICIAL CIRCUIT

You will see by the Journal that I have appointed to speak at Danville on the 22nd. of Sept.—the day after Douglas speaks there.

LETTER TO WILLIAM FITHIAN, SEPTEMBER 3, 1858

AUTUMN COLORS FILL THE STEEP BLUFFS ALONG THE MIDDLE FORK OF THE VERMILION RIVER
NEAR THE RIVER CROSSING OF THE OLD EIGHTH JUDICIAL CIRCUIT ROAD WEST OF DANVILLE, ILLINOIS.

You are in error if you suppose any important portion of my correspondence escapes my notice. Every thing requiring my action or attention is brought to my notice. No letter of yours, which has been received here, has been neglected or left unacknowledged.

LETTER TO WILLIAM H. FRY, JULY 19, 1862

According to Hiram Beckwith, Lincoln "relied on his well-trained memory that recorded and indexed every passing detail. And by his skillful questions, a joke, or pat retort, as the trial progressed, he steered his jury from the bayous and eddys of side issues and kept them clear of the snags and sandbars, if any were put in the real channel of his case." Lincoln was not, Beckwith recounted, "emotional and dramatic" like some colleagues on the circuit; he lacked "grace, music; nor were his thoughts set to words . . . in harmonic measure." His "shrill voice, in its higher tones, his stooping form, and long arms swinging about" made a poor first impression. "But all this either eluded notice, or was quickly forgot in the spell that radiated [from] his wonderful face and in the force of the words that came from his earnest lips." A casual observer "at once became an interested listener, and Mr. Lincoln's array of the law and fact was so easy, apt, and original that one was quickly in the drift of his argument and borne on by it fascinated to the end." Beckwith disagreed with those who maintained that Lincoln "in his earlier career was a mere 'case lawyer.'" To the contrary, "few, if any, practitioners were better, if as well, grounded in the elementary principles of the law. His knowledge of these, as well as the very reason for them, was so well mastered that he seemed to apply them to individual 'cases' as if by intuition." At that time, "law libraries were limited mostly to text books. Precedents of 'cases' reported from the higher courts" were relatively few. "Personal rights and remedies then lay more in the 'common law of the land' and less in statutory enactments. A mere 'case lawyer' would have had little chance either with Mr. Lincoln or his associates in the practice."

THE MIDDLE FORK OF THE VERMILION RIVER AT OR NEAR THE RIVER CROSSING OF THE OLD CIRCUIT ROAD WEST OF DANVILLE.

Following the Eighth Judicial Circuit

If my friend Dr. William Fithian, of Danville, Ill., should call on you, please give him such facilities as you consistently can about recovering the remains of a step-son and matters connected therewith. LETTER TO MAJOR-GENERAL SAMUEL R. CURTIS, DECEMBER 14, 1862

Yet we know all this exists even better than we could know an isolated fact upon the sworn testimony of one or two witnesses, just as we better know there is fire whence we see much smoke rising than could know it by one or two witnesses swearing to it. The witnesses may commit perjury, but the smoke can not.

DRAFT OF LETTER TO JOHN R. UNDERWOOD AND HENRY GRIDER, OCTOBER 26, 1864

William H. Fithian, a doctor who practiced throughout eastern Illinois, was Lincoln's friend, political ally, and client for over thirty years. The two served together in the Illinois General Assembly, where they championed the Whig legislative agenda. The doctor often hired Lincoln to represent him in various legal cases. In 1851, Lincoln won Fithian's suit against George W. Casseday, who falsely claimed that Fithian had abandoned his wife's corpse. The court awarded damages of $547.90. Thereafter, Casseday declared on his personal property tax schedule that among his possessions was the "character of Dr. Fithian, $547.90, which I bought and paid for." When in Danville on the circuit, Lincoln stayed at Fithian's home, and in 1858 he delivered a campaign address from the second story balcony of that residence. During the election campaign of 1860, Lincoln wrote to Fithian asking his help: "I appeal to you, because I can to no other with so much confidence."

A STEEP SECTION OF SHALE CLIFFS ALONG THE VERMILION RIVER WEST OF THE LOCATION WHERE
ABRAHAM LINCOLN CROSSED THE RIVER WHEN HEADING SOUTH FROM DANVILLE.

Abraham Lincoln stayed at the William Fithian home in Danville, Illinois, and made a speech from this balcony. The home is now the Vermilion County Museum.

A's father, with his own family & others mentioned, had, in pursuance of their intention, removed from Macon to Coles county. THIRD AUTOBIOGRAPHY

Owing to my father being left an orphan at the age of six years, in poverty, and in a new country, he became a wholly uneducated man; which I suppose is the reason why I know so little of our family history. LETTER TO SOLOMON LINCOLN, A DISTANT RELATIVE, MARCH 6, 1848

This is all I know certainly on the subject of names; it is, however, my father's understanding that, Abraham, Mordecai, and Thomas are old family names of ours. LETTER TO SOLOMON LINCOLN, A DISTANT RELATIVE, MARCH 24, 1848

A visitor to Thomas Lincoln's Coles County home found him residing "in a little cabin that cost perhaps $15, and with many evidences of poverty about him." The cabin "looked so small and humble" that the visitor "felt embarrassed." It had no stable, no outhouse, and no shrubbery or trees. There Thomas was barely able to eke out a living. An early historian of Coles County called Thomas "one of those easy, honest, commonplace men, who take life as they find it, and, as a consequence, generally find it a life of poverty." He "possessed no faculty whatever of preserving his money, when he made any, hence he always remained poor. He was easily contented, had few wants, and those of a primitive nature. He was a foe to intemperance, strictly honest, and, supposing others the same, often suffered pecuniary losses."

ABRAHAM LINCOLN VISITED HIS FATHER AND STEPMOTHER, THOMAS AND SARAH BUSH LINCOLN, AT THEIR FARMSTEAD NEAR LERNA, ILLINOIS. THEY ARE BOTH BURIED AT THE SHILOH CEMETERY A MILE AND A HALF WEST.

Sarah Bush, first married to Daniel Johnston, and afterwards second wife of Thos. Lincoln, was born Decr. 13th. 1788.

FAMILY RECORD WRITTEN BY ABRAHAM LINCOLN IN THOMAS LINCOLN'S FAMILY BIBLE, PROBABLY 1851

THE LOG CABIN AT LINCOLN LOG CABIN STATE HISTORIC SITE IS AN ACCURATE REPLICA ON THE ORIGINAL HOME SITE OF ABRAHAM LINCOLN'S FATHER AND STEPMOTHER'S FARM SOUTH OF CHARLESTON, ILLINOIS. THE LOG CABIN AND SURROUNDING FARMSTEAD WAS BUILT BY THE CIVILIAN CONSERVATION CORPS IN 1935.

My father, Thomas, is still living, in Coles county Illinois, being in the 71st. year of his age. His Post-office is Charleston, Coles co. Ill. I am his only child.

LETTER TO DAVID LINCOLN, A SECOND COUSIN, APRIL 2, 1848

My father (Thomas) died the 17th of January, 1851, in Coles County, Illinois, where he had resided twenty years. LETTER TO JESSE LINCOLN, ABRAHAM'S GRANDFATHER WAS JESSE'S UNCLE, APRIL 1, 1854

Lincoln and his stepmother were remarkably close. "I can say what scarcely one woman – a mother – can say in a thousand and it is this – Abe never gave me a cross word or look and never refused in fact, or Even in appearance, to do any thing I requested him," she remembered. In turn, she "never gave him a cross word." The two were kindred souls, she thought: "His mind & mine – what little I had [–] seemed to run together – move in the same channel." He "was dutiful to me always – he loved me truly I think." Abe, she said, "was the best boy I Ever Saw or Ever Expect to see." He "always wanted to do just as I wanted him."

Lincoln reciprocated the love of his stepmother. In 1861 he told a friend that "she had been his best Friend in this world & that no Son could love a Mother more than he loved her." Joshua Speed, Lincoln's closest confidant, recalled that his "fondness for his step-mother and his watchful care over her after the death of his father [in 1851] deserves notice. He could not bear to have any thing said by any one against her." Near the end of his life, Lincoln told Speed "of his affection for her and her kindness to him."

A SPLIT RAIL FENCE ON THE FARM OF THOMAS AND SARAH BUSH LINCOLN, LINCOLN LOG CABIN STATE HISTORIC SITE NEAR LERNA, ILLINOIS.

Thomas Lincoln, died, January 17 1851 aged 73 years & 11 days.

A NEW TEN INCHES OF SNOW COVERS THE THOMAS AND SARAH BUSH LINCOLN CABIN AND FARM SOUTH OF CHARLESTON, ILLINOIS. LINCOLN LOG CABIN STATE HISTORIC SITE IS AN ACTIVE LIVING HISTORY FARM AND MUSEUM.

Following the Eighth Judicial Circuit

I have been absent on the circuit seven weeks, only getting home to the election; so that I could not answer your letter of the 16th. of Octr. till now.

LETTER TO ISAAC ONSTOTT, NOVEMBER 6, 1850

THE KASKASKIA RIVER DURING LOW WATER NEAR SULLIVAN, ILLINOIS. ABRAHAM LINCOLN CROSSED THE RIVER NEAR THIS LOCATION TRAVELING THE OLD CIRCUIT ROAD. THE KASKASKIA IS THE SECOND LARGEST RIVER SYSTEM IN ILLINOIS.

Your letter reached here a day or two after I started on the circuit; I was gone five or six weeks, so that I got the letter only a few days before Butler started to your country.　　LETTER TO JOSHUA SPEED, JULY 4, 1842

I reached home from the circuit yesterday, after an absence; and hence your letter of May the 8th. was not sooner answered.

LETTER TO ORVILLE H. BROWNING AND NEHEMIAH BUSHNELL, JUNE 5, 1851

Until 1853, when the boundaries of the Eighth Judicial Circuit were altered, Taylorville was known as "the last stop."

The courthouse was raised above ground on blocks. During one trial there, Lincoln allegedly asked Judge David Davis

to issue a "writ of quietus" to silence the hogs who were noisily wallowing around beneath the building.

THE TAYLORVILLE COURTHOUSE IS THE ONLY ORIGINAL WOODEN FRAMED COURTHOUSE IN ILLINOIS STILL IN EXISTENCE
WHERE ABRAHAM LINCOLN PRACTICED LAW. THE COURTHOUSE HAS BEEN MOVED FROM ITS ORIGINAL LOCATION
ON THE TAYLORVILLE SQUARE TO THE CHRISTIAN COUNTY HISTORICAL SOCIETY MUSEUM.

CAMPAIGNING FOR WHIGS

Always a whig in politics, and generally on the whig electoral tickets, making active canvasses.

SECOND AUTOBIOGRAPHY

. . . spent much time and labor in both those canvasses.

THIRD AUTOBIOGRAPHY

James Ratcliff, known as "Old Beaver" for his energetic nature, had the Stagecoach Inn erected in 1828. In 1840, Lincoln allegedly stayed here while stumping throughout southern Illinois on behalf of the Whig party. The hardships of campaigning in such a primitive region were compounded by illness. As Lincoln traveled from town to town, he found himself "shaking with the ague one day, and addressing the people the next." In the absence of railroads and stage lines, he had to ride on horseback with his clothes jammed into saddlebags. He covered vast distances through swamp and over prairie all the while enduring miserable accommodations (the Stagecoach Inn was an exception).

ABRAHAM LINCOLN STAYED IN THE HOME OF COLONEL WILLIAM JONES WHILE CAMPAIGNING FOR WHIG PRESIDENTIAL CANDIDATE HENRY CLAY NEAR HIS BOYHOOD HOME IN 1844, COLONEL WILLIAM JONES STATE HISTORIC SITE, GENTRYVILLE, INDIANA.

... canvassing quite fully his own district in Illinois ...

THIRD AUTOBIOGRAPHY

ABRAHAM LINCOLN LODGED AT THE RATCLIFF INN IN CARMI, ILLINOIS, AN OLD STAGECOACH TAVERN,
WHILE CAMPAIGNING FOR WHIG PRESIDENTIAL CANDIDATE WILLIAM HENRY HARRISON IN 1840.
THE RATCLIFF INN MUSEUM IS OPERATED BY THE WHITE COUNTY HISTORICAL SOCIETY.

ELECTED TO THE U.S. CONGRESS

In 1846 I was once elected to the lower House of Congress. SECOND AUTOBIOGRAPHY

ABOVE: ABRAHAM LINCOLN SERVED AS A REPRESENTATIVE OF ILLINOIS IN THE 30TH CONGRESS OF THE UNITED STATES
AT THE U.S. CAPITOL IN WASHINGTON, D.C. FOR TWO YEARS. (NATIONAL HISTORIC LANDMARK)

FOLLOWING PAGE: CONSTRUCTION OF THE WASHINGTON MONUMENT NATIONAL MONUMENT BEGAN IN 1848
WHILE ABRAHAM LINCOLN WAS IN THE 30TH CONGRESS. WORK STOPPED IN 1854 AND DIDN'T RESUME UNTIL 1879.
WHEN LINCOLN WAS PRESIDENT, HE VIEWED A PARTIALLY BUILT MONUMENT. THIS PERIOD OF YEARS CAN BE SEEN
IN THE COLOR OF THE STONE ABOUT A THIRD OF THE WAY UP THE OBELISK—THE WORLD'S TALLEST STONE STRUCTURE.

When the cornerstone of the Washington Monument was dedicated on July 4, 1848, Lincoln, who was in the nation's capital serving as a congressman from Illinois, may have attended the ceremony. The monument, which is 555 feet tall, was not completed until 1884.

What did he and Eddy think of the little letters father sent them? Don't let the blessed fellows forget father.
LETTER TO MARY TODD LINCOLN, APRIL 16, 1848

In 1847, the capitol did not resemble the building pictured here. It was surmounted by a wooden dome and lacked the wings it would eventually acquire. At that time Washington was little more than an "an ill-contrived, ill-arranged, rambling, scrambling village" with a population of 40,000. Europeans expressed scorn for the capital, which reminded an Englishwoman "of a vast plantation with houses purposely kept far apart to give them room to grow and spread." Eminent British novelists were especially critical. Charles Dickens described it as "the head-quarters of tobacco-tinctured saliva," a "City of Magnificent Intentions," with "spacious avenues, that begin in nothing, and lead nowhere; streets, miles-long, that only want houses, roads, and inhabitants; public buildings that need but a public to be complete." Anthony Trollope wrote in 1862: "Of all places that I know it is the most ungainly," the "most unsatisfactory," and "the most presumptuous in its pretensions."

Some Americans were also taken aback by their capital. A Bostonian protested that Washington "covers too much ground to generate a cheerful spirit, for vastness is repellent to the social pleasure of unceremonious visiting." Moreover, it lacked "the native aristocracy of wealth or talent to be found in the commercial cities." In 1854, Carl Schurz described the capital as "a strange-looking city. Imagine a broad street lined on both sides with hotels and shops, then wide stretches of open country and again streets interrupted by vacant lots; groups of houses scattered about in apparent disorder, with here and there a marble palace which contains one of the Government Departments. This strange jumble leaves the spectator in doubt whether all this grandeur is in a state of development or is already approaching decay."

ELECTED TO THE U.S. CONGRESS

In 1846, he was elected to the lower House of Congress, and served one term only, commencing in Dec. 1847 and ending with the inauguration of Gen. Taylor, in March 1849.

THIRD AUTOBIOGRAPHY

Like scenes in some enchanted isle,
All bathed in liquid light.
As distant mountains please the eye,
When twilight chases day—
As bugle-tones, that, passing by,
In distance die away—
As leaving some grand water-fall
We ling'ring, list it's roar,

EXCERPT FROM THE POEM "MY CHILDHOOD-HOME I SEE AGAIN", 1846

Niagara-Falls! By what mysterious power is it that millions and millions, are drawn from all parts of the world, to gaze upon Niagara Falls? ... Yet this is really a very small part of that world's wonder. It's power to excite reflection, and emotion, is it's great charm. ...

"NIAGARA FALLS", UNFINISHED MEDITATION, SEPTEMBER, 1848

In 1858, William Herndon visited Niagara Falls and upon his return enthused to Lincoln about the site's beauty and grandeur. Lincoln disappointed Herndon with his response: "The thing that struck me most forcibly when I saw the Falls was, where in the world did all that water come from?" Herndon concluded from this remark that Lincoln had no appreciation for the sublime. But clearly Lincoln was pulling his partner's leg, for the private, incomplete memo he wrote about Niagara's grandeur (above and page 158) was unknown to Herndon.

ABRAHAM LINCOLN FIRST VISITED NIAGARA FALLS ON HIS RETURN TRIP HOME AFTER SERVING IN CONGRESS.
HE VISITED AMERICAN FALLS ON THIS TRIP IN SEPTEMBER, 1848, LATER WRITING THE MEDITATION ABOVE AND ON PAGE 158.
HIS WRITING CONVEYS HIS WONDER AT EXPERIENCING THE FALLS.

ABRAHAM LINCOLN VISITED AMERICAN FALLS WITH HIS FAMILY, AFTER TRAVELING FROM BOSTON, BEFORE BOARDING A STEAMSHIP FROM BUFFALO TO DETROIT. NIAGARA FALLS STATE PARK IS THE OLDEST STATE PARK IN THE UNITED STATES. (NATIONAL HISTORIC LANDMARK)

Elected to the U.S. Congress

Niagara-Falls! . . . It's power to excite reflection, and emotion, is it's great charm.

"Niagara Falls", unfinished meditation, September, 1848

But still there is more. It calls up the indefinite past. When Columbus first sought this continent—when Christ suffered on the cross—when Moses led Israel through the Red-Sea—nay, even, when Adam first came from the hand of his Maker—then as now, Niagara was roaring here. The eyes of that species of extinct giants, whose bones fill the mounds of America, have gazed on Niagara, as ours do now. Co[n]temporary with the whole race of men, and older than the first man, Niagara is strong, and fresh to-day as ten thousand years ago. The Mammoth and Mastadon—now so long dead, that fragments of their monstrous bones, alone testify, that they ever lived, have gazed on Niagara. In that long—long time, never still for a single moment. Never dried, never froze, never slept, never rested,

Last paragraph of "Niagara Falls", unfinished meditation, September, 1848

Get another as soon as you can to take charge of the dear codgers. Father expected to see you all sooner; but let it pass; stay as long as you please, and come when you please. Kiss and love the dear rascals.

Affectionately A. Lincoln

Letter to Mary Todd Lincoln, July 2, 1848

Abraham and Mary Lincoln visited Niagara Falls a second time on a trip to New York City in July, 1857. They visited American Falls and also Horseshoe Falls in Canada on this trip.

When Abraham Lincoln marveled at Niagara Falls, more than twice the volume of water flowed over the falls than flows present day in peak season. (National Historic Landmark)

Practicing the Law in Communities Outside the Circuit

My way of living leads me to be about the courts of justice;

SPEECH IN U.S. HOUSE OF REPRESENTATIVES, JANUARY 12, 1848

AS WITH MANY LOCATIONS ABRAHAM LINCOLN VISITED, HUMOROUS STORIES ABOUND—ON THE LIST IS
THE JOHN SHASTID HOUSE IN PITTSFIELD, ILLINOIS. SHASTID WAS AN OLD NEW SALEM FRIEND
AND THE HOME IS NOW A MUSEUM OPERATED BY THE PIKE COUNTY HISTORICAL SOCIETY.

I am to examine this & have Mr. Hay write the writer.

Milton Hay read law at the Lincoln-Herndon office at night and helped Lincoln by copying briefs and declarations. A cheerful, tobacco-chewing, imposing figure with a forehead like Daniel Webster's, Hay became a leading member of the Illinois bar.

The journalist John Russell Young described John Hay as he appeared during his years as Lincoln's assistant private secretary: "brilliant" and "chivalrous," quite "independent, with opinions on most questions," which he expressed freely. At times sociable, Hay could also be "reserved" and aloof, "with just a shade of pride that did not make acquaintanceship spontaneous." Hay, Young said, combined "the genius for romance and politics as no one . . . since Disraeli," and judged that he was well "suited for his place in the President's family." Young depicted Hay as "a comely young man with [a] peach-blossom face," "exceedingly handsome – a slight, graceful, boyish figure – 'girl in boy's clothes,' as I heard in a sniff from some angry politician." This youthful, "almost beardless, and almost boyish countenance did not seem to match with official responsibilities and the tumult of action in time of pressure, but he did what he had to do, was always graceful, composed, polite, and equal to the complexities of any situation which might arise." Hay's "old-fashioned speech" was "smooth, low-toned, quick in comprehension, sententious, reserved." People were "not quite sure whether it was the reserve of diffidence or aristocracy," Young remembered. The "high-bred, courteous" Hay was "not one with whom the breezy overflowing politician would be apt to take liberties." Young noticed "a touch of sadness in his temperament" and concluded that Hay "had the personal attractiveness as well as the youth of Byron."

THE MILTON HAY HOUSE IN PITTSFIELD WAS HOME TO ABRAHAM LINCOLN'S ASSISTANT PRIVATE SECRETARY, JOHN HAY. JOHN LIVED HERE WHILE ATTENDING THE THOMPSON ACADEMY. HE MET LINCOLN THROUGH HIS UNCLE MILTON HAY, WHO HAD BEEN A STUDENT OF LINCOLN'S, AND LATER HAD A LAW OFFICE NEXT DOOR TO LINCOLN'S LAW OFFICE IN SPRINGFIELD.

I write this to appologise for not being with you to-day. I was forced off to Pike county, where I spoke yesterday, and I have just returned. LETTER TO JAMES M. RUGGLE, OCTOBER 28, 1856

ABRAHAM LINCOLN STAYED AT THE HOME OF COLONEL WILLIAM ROSS, THE FOUNDER OF PITTSFIELD, DURING HIS SENATORIAL CAMPAIGN VISIT TO PITTSFIELD, ILLINOIS.

But to return to your position: Allow the President to invade a neighboring nation, whenever he shall deem it necessary to repel an invasion, and you allow him to do so, whenever he may choose to say he deems it necessary for such purpose—and you allow him to make war at pleasure. . . .

The provision of the Constitution giving the war-making power to Congress, was dictated, as I understand it, by the following reasons. Kings had always been involving and impoverishing their people in wars, pretending generally, if not always, that the good of the people was the object. This, our Convention understood to be the most oppressive of all Kingly oppressions; and they resolved to so frame the Constitution that no one man should hold the power of bringing this oppression upon us. But your view destroys the whole matter, and places our President where kings have always stood.   LETTER TO WILLIAM H. HERNDON, FEBRUARY 15, 1848

The Ross house was built in the mid-1840s and rebuilt half a century later. A leading citizen of Pittsfield, William Ross served with Lincoln during the Black Hawk War in 1832 and later with him in the Illinois General Assembly. In 1860, Ross, as a delegate at the Chicago convention, helped Lincoln win the Republican presidential nomination. Lincoln spent the night of September 30, 1858, at the Ross house and delivered a speech in Pittsfield the following day.

Michael Noyes settled in Pittsfield in 1841 and immediately established the town's first newspaper. According to Noyes family history, Lincoln once delivered a speech on the front lawn of the Noyes house. (That was perhaps in 1856, when Lincoln visited Pittsfield and spoke on behalf of Republican presidential candidate John C. Fremont.)

ABRAHAM LINCOLN GAVE A SPEECH IN THE YARD OF THE MICHAEL NOYES HOME IN PITTSFIELD.
NOYES WAS THE FOUNDER AND EDITOR OF PIKE COUNTY'S FIRST NEWSPAPER, THE SUCKER AND FARMER'S RECORD.

Look up the old Almanac & other data and see if I am not right. A. Lincoln

LETTER TO SECRETARY OF WAR EDWIN STANTON, MARCH 27, 1865

I repeat that if Trumbull had himself been in the plot, it would not at all relieve the others who were in it from blame. If I should be indicted for murder, and upon the trial it should be discovered that I had been implicated in that murder, but that the prosecuting witness was guilty too, that would not at all touch the question of my crime. It would be no relief to my neck that they discovered this other man who charged the crime upon me to be guilty too.

FOURTH LINCOLN-DOUGLAS DEBATE AT CHARLESTON, SEPTEMBER 18, 1858

Again, a jury too frequently have at least one member, more ready to hang the panel than to hang the traitor.

LETTER TO ERASTUS CORNING AND OTHERS, [JUNE 12], 1863

The 1844 Beardstown Courthouse, which to this day sits on the town square, contains one of only two courtrooms still in use where Lincoln argued cases. His most famous case there was the 1858 "Almanac Trial," when Lincoln defended Duff Armstrong, who was charged with murder. Two decades earlier, Duff's parents had been generous friends of Lincoln when he lived in New Salem. At the trial, Lincoln used an 1857 almanac to discredit the testimony of the star prosecution witness, who alleged that he had seen Duff commit the murder by the light of the full moon at 11 p.m. The almanac showed that moon, instead of being high overhead at 11 p.m., was low on the horizon and due to set within an hour. The jury acquitted Duff.

THE COURTROOM IN THE BEARDSTOWN COURTHOUSE IS THE LOCATION OF LINCOLN'S FAMOUS ALMANAC TRIAL.
IN THIS COURTROOM HE DEFENDED DUFF ARMSTRONG, THE SON OF JACK ARMSTRONG, A CLOSE FRIEND FROM HIS NEW SALEM YEARS.

The Beardstown Courthouse in Beardstown, Illinois, is one of only two original courthouses where Abraham Lincoln practiced law which is still used as a courthouse and city hall. It is also home to the Old Lincoln Courtroom & Museum.

My expectation is to be at the Mount-Vernon Supreme Court, reaching there the 21st. of the month.

LETTER TO MICHAEL G. DALE, NOVEMBER 8, 1859

In 1841, William B. Archer, a friend and political ally of Lincoln as well as the founder of the town of Marshall, built the Archer House, the oldest hotel in Illinois.

As a delegate to the 1856 Republican National Convention, Congressman Archer resolved to nominate Lincoln for Vice-President. He lined up support for his friend and asked a fellow congressman from Pennsylvania, John Allison, to nominate Lincoln. Allison did so, describing Lincoln as a "prince of good fellows, and an Old-Line Whig." Seconding the nomination, Archer declared that he "had been acquainted with the man who had been named for 30 years. He had lived in Illinois 40 years. He had gone there when Illinois was a Territory, and had lived there until it had grown to be a populous and flourishing State. During thirty years of that time, he had known Abraham Lincoln, and he knew him well. He was born in gallant Kentucky, and was now in the prime of life . . . and enjoying remarkable good health. And, besides, the speaker knew him to be as pure a patriot as ever lived. He would give the Convention to understand, that with him on the ticket, there was no danger of Northern Illinois. Illinois was safe with him, and he believed she was safe without him. With him, however, she was doubly safe." Suddenly an Ohio delegate interrupted Archer, shouting out: "Will he fight?" To the amusement of the delegates, Archer, "a grey-haired old gent, slightly bent with age," then "jumped straight from the floor, as high as the Secretaries' table, and cried out, shrill and wild, 'Yes.'" The delegates were "convulsed, and a tremendous yell of approbation substantially inserted a fighting plank in the platform."

ABRAHAM LINCOLN STAYED IN THE ARCHER HOUSE, AN OLD STAGECOACH INN AT MARSHALL, ILLINOIS, WHILE PRACTICING LAW AT THE CLARK COUNTY COURTHOUSE. (NATIONAL HISTORIC LANDMARK)

After 1848, the Illinois Supreme Court met in Mt. Vernon and Ottawa as well as Springfield. Now and then, Lincoln would travel to Mt. Vernon to attend the sessions of the Supreme Court (most notably in 1859 when he argued the important case of the State of Illinois v. Illinois Central Railroad), but most of his work before that body took place in Springfield.

THE APPELLATE COURTHOUSE IN MT. VERNON, ILLINOIS, IS ONE OF ONLY TWO ORIGINAL COURTHOUSES
WHERE ABRAHAM LINCOLN PRACTICED LAW WHICH IS STILL USED AS A COURTHOUSE.
WHEN LINCOLN WORKED ON A CASE HERE IN 1859, IT WAS THE ILLINOIS SUPREME COURT.

COMPELLED TO REENTER POLITICS

I was losing interest in politics, when the repeal of the Missouri Compromise aroused me again.

SECOND AUTOBIOGRAPHY

In the canvass of 1856, Mr. L. made over fifty speeches, no one of which, so far as he remembers, was put in print. One of them was made at Galena, but Mr. L. has no recollection of any part of it being printed;

THIRD AUTOBIOGRAPHY

In 1856, Lincoln threw himself into the presidential campaign, delivering over fifty speeches around Illinois during an unusually bitter and violent campaign. His principal concern was to woo disaffected Whigs, who regarded the Republican candidate, John C. Fremont, as a dangerous abolitionist. At Galena, Lincoln rejected the charge of sectionalism leveled against the Republicans, a charge he called "the most difficult objection we have to meet." The "naked issue" that divided the Democrats from his party he summarized briefly: "Shall slavery be allowed to extend into U.S. territory, now legally free?" Appealing to fair-minded voters, he asked "how is one side of this question, more sectional than the other?" If the parties were, like most other institutions, divided along sectional lines, how should the problem be solved? The answer was simple, he declared: one side must yield. Republicans "boldly say, let all who really think slavery ought to spread into free territory, openly go over against us." But why, he asked, should anyone who opposed slavery vote Democratic? "Do they really think the right ought to yield to the wrong? Are they afraid to stand by the right? Do they really think that by right surrendering to wrong, the hopes of our Constitution, our Union, and our liberties, can possibly be bettered?"

THE DESOTO HOUSE HOTEL IS THE OLDEST OPERATING HOTEL IN ILLINOIS. GALENA WAS ULYSSES S. GRANT'S HOME WHEN THE CIVIL WAR BEGAN. AFTER THE WAR, THE HOTEL BECAME GRANT'S PRESIDENTIAL CAMPAIGN HEADQUARTERS IN 1868. ALONG WITH BEING A QUALITY HOTEL, THE DESOTO HOUSE CELEBRATES ITS LONG HISTORY WITH FEATURES OF A MUSEUM.

"But the Union, in any event, won't be dissolved. We don't want to dissolve it, and if you attempt it, we won't let you. . . . All this talk about the dissolution of the Union is humbug—nothing but folly. We "wont" dissolve the Union, and you "shant"."

CONCLUSION OF SPEECH AT GALENA, JULY 23, 1856
SIMILAR ENDING TO THE "LOST SPEECH" MADE MAY 29 IN BLOOMINGTON
REPORTED IN GALENA NEWSPAPER, THE WEEKLY NORTHWESTERN GAZETTE

You don't know what you are talking about, my friend. I am quite willing to answer any gentleman in the crowd who asks an intelligent question. SPEECH AT CHICAGO, JULY 10, 1858

ABRAHAM LINCOLN GAVE A SPEECH FROM THE FRONT OUTSIDE BALCONY OF THE DeSOTO HOUSE HOTEL
TO A LARGE CROWD IN THE STREET BELOW WHILE CAMPAIGNING FOR REPUBLICAN PRESIDENTIAL CANDIDATE JOHN FREMONT.

Compelled to Reenter Politics

In 1854, his profession had almost superseded the thought of politics in his mind, when the repeal of the Missouri compromise aroused him as he had never been before.

THIRD AUTOBIOGRAPHY

ABOVE: ABRAHAM LINCOLN STAYED ONE NIGHT IN THE TALLMAN HOUSE, A MANSION IN JANESVILLE, WISCONSIN, WHILE DELIVERING SPEECHES IN THE STATE. THE HOUSE IS NOW A MUSEUM OPERATED BY THE ROCK COUNTY HISTORICAL SOCIETY.

FOLLOWING PAGE: THE NACHUSA HOUSE HOTEL HAS A LONG HISTORY AND IS ON THE U.S. NATIONAL REGISTER OF HISTORIC PLACES. LINCOLN CERTAINLY SAW THE FORMER HOTEL DIRECTLY ACROSS FROM THE COURTHOUSE WHILE SPEAKING IN DIXON, ILLINOIS, BUT CONTRARY TO TRADITION, NO EVIDENCE SHOWS THAT HE STAYED IN THE HOTEL.

... I was very careful not to put anything in that speech as a matter of fact, or make any inferences which did not appear to me to be true, and fully warrantable. If I had made any mistake I was willing to be corrected; if I had drawn any inference in regard to Judge Douglas, or any one else, which was not warranted, I was fully prepared to modify it as soon as discovered. I planted myself upon the truth, and the truth only, so far as I knew it, or could be brought to know it.... I set out in this campaign, with the intention of conducting it strictly as a gentleman, in substance at least, if not in the outside polish. The latter I shall never be, but that which constitutes the inside of a gentleman I hope I understand, and am not less inclined to practice than others. [CHEERS] It was my purpose and expectations that this canvass would be conducted upon principle, and with fairness on both sides; and it shall not be my fault, if this purpose and expectation shall be given up.

SPEECH AT SPRINGFIELD, JULY 17, 1858

In 1859, Lincoln stumped through Wisconsin, speaking at Milwaukee, Beloit, and Janesville. Between 1855 and 1857, William Morrison Tallman, a lawyer, land speculator, real estate developer, and abolitionist, built the Tallman House, the only surviving private residence in Wisconsin where Lincoln spent the night. The mansion contains the bed that Lincoln slept on during his visit.

In his Wisconsin speeches, Lincoln extolled the advantages of free labor and refuted what he called "the 'mud-sill' theory" propounded by Southerners like George Fitzhugh and James H. Hammond. Labor, he argued, "is prior to, and independent of, capital," for "capital is the fruit of labor" and therefore "labor is the superior – greatly superior – of capital." The free labor system, in which the "prudent, penniless beginner in the world, labors for wages awhile, saves a surplus with which to buy tools or land, for himself; then labors on his own account another while, and at length hires another new beginner to help," is "the just and generous, and prosperous system, which opens the way for all – gives hope to all, and energy, and progress, and improvement of condition to all."

The Debates with Douglas

Will it be agreeable to you to make an arrangement for you and myself to divide time, and address the same audiences during the present canvass?

Letter challenging Stephen A. Douglas to debates, July 24, 1858

Douglas stayed at the Bryant Cottage in late July 1858. While there, he wrote to Lincoln accepting a challenge to hold debates during the remainder of their heated campaign for the U.S. Senate. The tradition that the two men met at the cottage to arrange the debates is not supported by extant evidence. On July 24, when Lincoln saw the published announcement of Douglas's appointments for August, he conferred with Norman B. Judd about debating his opponent. Judd, sensing that Lincoln had already determined to challenge the senator, said he thought it would be a good idea. Lincoln then wrote a letter for Judd to deliver to Douglas, formally proposing that they "divide time, and address the same audiences." With great difficulty, Judd tracked Douglas down. When, after three days, he finally did catch up with him and presented Lincoln's note, the Little Giant angrily asked: "What do you come to me with such a thing as this for?" He berated Judd for abandoning the Democratic party. Ignoring the insults, Judd handed over Lincoln's challenge, which Douglas "angrily and emphatically declined to consider on the ground that it was a childish idea and that he would be belittling himself and dignifying Lincoln." Judd warned Douglas that if he refused to debate, he would seem afraid of his rival. Fearing to appear like a coward, Douglas agreed to participate in seven debates.

LEFT: REDBUD TREES IN BLOOM AT BRYANT COTTAGE STATE HISTORICAL SITE IN BEMENT, ILLINOIS.

RIGHT: THIS PORTRAIT OF ABRAHAM LINCOLN WAS PROBABLY MADE IN SPRINGFIELD OR PEORIA IN 1858.

In his numerous speeches now being made in Illinois, Senator Douglas regularly argues against the doctrine of the equality of men; and while he does not draw the conclusion that the superiors ought to enslave the inferiors, he evidently wishes his hearers to draw that conclusion. He shirks the responsibility of pulling the house down, but he digs under it that it may fall of its own weight. NOTES FOR SPEECHES, OCTOBER 1, 1858

WHILE STEPHEN DOUGLAS STAYED IN THIS HOME IN BEMENT, ILLINOIS, HE WROTE ABRAHAM LINCOLN ACCEPTING THE PROPOSED DEBATES AND SETTING THE STAGE FOR THE SEVEN LINCOLN-DOUGLAS SENATORIAL DEBATES, BRYANT COTTAGE STATE HISTORICAL SITE.

The Debates with Douglas

At Galesburg, I tried to show that by the Dred Scott Decision, pushed to its legitimate consequences, slavery would be established in all the States as well as in the Territories. SIXTH LINCOLN-DOUGLAS DEBATE AT QUINCY, OCTOBER 13, 1858

THE EAST SIDE OF OLD MAIN AT KNOX COLLEGE IN GALESBURG, ILLINOIS, THE SITE OF THE FIFTH LINCOLN-DOUGLAS DEBATE. OLD MAIN IS THE ONLY ORIGINAL STRUCTURE STILL REMAINING AT ANY OF THE LINCOLN-DOUGLAS DEBATE SITES. (NATIONAL HISTORIC LANDMARK)

I see it rapidly approaching. Whatever may be the result of this ephemeral contest between Judge Douglas and myself, I see the day rapidly approaching when his pill of sectionalism, which he has been thrusting down the throats of Republicans for years past, will be crowded down his own throat.

FIFTH LINCOLN-DOUGLAS DEBATE AT GALESBURG, OCTOBER 7, 1858

On October 7, 1858, Lincoln and Douglas met at Galesburg, a Republican town 175 miles southwest of Chicago, where they clashed for the fifth time. It drew the biggest crowd of the seven debates. Abolitionism flourished at Knox College, where the candidates addressed the audience from a platform adjacent to Old Main, the largest structure on campus. (To reach that platform, speakers and dignitaries had to enter the building, walk down a corridor, then step through a window. After Lincoln did so, he quipped: "At last I have gone through college.") Though the sun shone, cold temperatures and high winds made for a disagreeable day. The central issue dividing the parties, Lincoln maintained, was the morality of slavery. Douglas and his friends denied "that there is any wrong in slavery." The Republicans disagreed. Lincoln declared that he belonged "to that class in the country who contemplate slavery as a moral, social, and political evil" and who "desire a policy that looks to the prevention of it as a wrong, and looks hopefully to the time when as a wrong it may come to an end."

LEFT: THE STAGE FOR THE FIFTH LINCOLN-DOUGLAS DEBATE WAS SET UP DIRECTLY IN FRONT OF THE DOORS ON THE EAST SIDE OF OLD MAIN AT KNOX COLLEGE BECAUSE OF HIGH WINDS FROM THE WEST. WITH THE STAGE BLOCKING THE DOORS, LINCOLN AND DOUGLAS HAD TO ACCESS THE PLATFORM BY CLIMBING THROUGH THE WINDOW ON THE LEFT.

RIGHT: OLD MAIN AT KNOX COLLEGE IN GALESBURG AT FIRST LIGHT.

The Debates with Douglas

They lie side by side, the Mississippi river only dividing them;

SPEECH IN PEORIA, OCTOBER 16, 1854

VIEW SOUTH OF THE PALISADES ON THE MISSISSIPPI RIVER NEAR GRAFTON, ILLINOIS, NORTH OF ALTON, WITH MISSOURI TO THE RIGHT. LINCOLN TRAVELED THIS STRETCH OF RIVER SEVERAL TIMES BY WOODEN FLATBOAT AND YEARS LATER BY STEAMBOAT.

Stand with anybody that stands right. Stand with him while he is right and part with him when he goes wrong. . . .

If the ordinance of '87 did not keep slavery out of the north west territory, how happens it that the north west shore of the Ohio river is entirely free from it; while the south east shore, less than a mile distant, along nearly the whole length of the river, is entirely covered with it?

If that ordinance did not keep it out of Illinois, what was it that made the difference between Illinois and Missouri? They lie side by side, the Mississippi river only dividing them; while their early settlements were within the same latitude.
SPEECH FOLLOWING DOUGLAS, PEORIA, OCTOBER 16, 1854

At the final debate, held in Alton, Lincoln summed up the basic issue underlying his approach to slavery and Douglas's. The morality of slavery, he insisted, was the crux of the matter: "That is the real issue. That is the issue that will continue in this country when these poor tongues of Judge Douglas and myself shall be silent. It is the eternal struggle between these two principles – right and wrong – throughout the world. They are the two principles that have stood face to face from the beginning of time, and will ever continue to struggle. The one is the common right of humanity, and the other the 'divine right of kings.' It is the same principle in whatever shape it develops itself. It is the same spirit that says, 'You work and toil and earn bread, and I'll eat it.' [Loud applause.] No matter in what shape it comes, whether from the mouth of a king who seeks to bestride the people of his own nation and live by the fruit of their labor, or from one race of men as an apology for enslaving another race, it is the same tyrannical principle."

SUNSET ON THE MISSISSIPPI RIVER NORTH OF ALTON, LOOKING WEST INTO MISSOURI. ABRAHAM LINCOLN TRAVELED THE RIVER FROM QUINCY TO ALTON BY PADDLE STEAMER FOR THE LAST LINCOLN-DOUGLAS DEBATE.

THE COOPER INSTITUTE AND NEW ENGLAND

When I reached New York, I, for the first [time], learned that the place was changed to "Cooper Institute." I made the speech, and left for New Hampshire, where I have a son at school, neither asking for pay nor having any offered me.

LETTER TO CORNELIUS F. McNEIL, APRIL 6, 1860

THIS PORTRAIT OF ABRAHAM LINCOLN WAS MADE BY MATHEW B. BRADY AT HIS STUDIO IN NEW YORK CITY ON THE AFTERNOON OF FEBRUARY 27, 1860, ONLY HOURS BEFORE LINCOLN DELIVERED HIS ADDRESS AT THE COOPER INSTITUTE (NOW THE COOPER UNION). LINCOLN'S SPEECH WAS ENTHUSIASTICALLY RECEIVED IN NEW YORK CITY AND IMMEDIATELY WIDELY PUBLISHED ALONG WITH THIS PHOTOGRAPH. BOTH WERE INSTRUMENTAL IN LEADING TO LINCOLN BECOMING PRESIDENT.

Holding, as they do, that slavery is morally right, and socially elevating, they cannot cease to demand a full national recognition of it, as a legal right, and a social blessing. Nor can we justifiably withhold this, on any ground save our conviction that slavery is wrong.

. . . Let us have faith that right makes might, and in that faith, let us, to the end, dare to do our duty as we understand it.

ADDRESS AT COOPER INSTITUTE, NEW YORK CITY, FEBRUARY 27, 1860

At Cooper Union, Lincoln elaborately refuted Stephen A. Douglas's claim that the Founders of the nation did not intend to empower Congress to prohibit the expansion of slavery into the western territories. In a brilliant piece of historical research and analysis, he examined the views of the signers of the Constitution as manifested in votes on many pieces of legislation and showed that Douglas was manifestly wrong. Lincoln also addressed remarks to Southern whites, urging them to stop their insults and to deal rationally with their opponents' arguments. He counseled Republicans to remain forbearing in the face of Southern extortion and other provocations. In a mighty crescendo, Lincoln concluded: "Let us have faith that right makes might, and in that faith, let us, to the end, dare to do our duty as we understand it." During these closing remarks, which one auditor called "perfectly electrical," the audience "could hear the gentle sizzling of the gas-burners. When he reached a climax, the thunders of applause were terrific." One auditor shouted like a "wild Indian" and proclaimed Lincoln "the greatest man since St. Paul." Another said he "never saw an audience more thoroughly carried away by an orator."

THE COOPER INSTITUTE (NOW THE COOPER UNION) IN LOWER MANHATTAN OF NEW YORK CITY AT SUNRISE.
(NATIONAL HISTORIC LANDMARK)

THE COOPER INSTITUTE AND NEW ENGLAND

The speech at New York, being within my calculation before I started, went off passably well and gave me no trouble whatever. The difficulty was to make nine others, before reading audiences who had already seen all my ideas in print.

LETTER TO MARY TODD LINCOLN, MARCH 4, 1860

In all matters but this of Slavery the framers of the Constitution used the very clearest, shortest, and most direct language. But the Constitution alludes to Slavery three times without mentioning it once! The language used becomes ambiguous, roundabout, and mystical.   SPEECH AT NEW HAVEN, CONNECTICUT, MARCH 6, 1860

ABRAHAM LINCOLN GAVE A VERY INFLUENTIAL POLITICAL SPEECH IN THIS ROOM, THE GREAT HALL OF THE COOPER UNION
IN NEW YORK CITY. IT LED TO A SERIES OF SPEAKING EVENTS THROUGHOUT NEW ENGLAND
AND LED TO LINCOLN BECOMING A NATIONALLY-RECOGNIZED REPUBLICAN LEADER.

THE COOPER INSTITUTE (NOW THE COOPER UNION) IN NEW YORK CITY HAS A DISTINGUISHED HISTORY.
IN LINCOLN'S TIME, IT WAS A PREEMINENT SPEAKING ARENA. THE COLLEGE IS LOCATED IN THE
EAST VILLAGE OF LOWER MANHATTAN IN NEW YORK CITY. (NATIONAL HISTORIC LANDMARK)

THE COOPER INSTITUTE AND NEW ENGLAND

Friday we came down to Lawrence . . . where we remained four hours awaiting the train back to Exeter. When it came, we went upon it to Exeter where the boys got off, and I went on to Dover and spoke there Friday evening.

LETTER TO MARY TODD LINCOLN, MARCH 4, 1860

ABRAHAM LINCOLN VISITED HIS SON ROBERT AT PHILLIPS EXETER ACADEMY WHERE HE WAS ATTENDING SCHOOL.
LINCOLN'S VISIT TO EXETER HELPED ESTABLISH HIS GROWING POPULARITY IN THE NORTHEAST.

This is Sunday morning; and according to Bob's orders, I am to go to church once to-day. LETTER TO MARY TODD LINCOLN, MARCH 4, 1860

Lincoln's success at Cooper Union led to many speaking invitations from Republicans in New England. He had originally intended to visit his son Robert at Phillips Exeter Academy in New Hampshire and then return to Springfield promptly, but he agreed to take to the stump in the Granite State, in Rhode Island, and in Connecticut, where state elections were scheduled that April. During the first two weeks of March, Lincoln gave hastily-scheduled addresses in Providence and Woonsocket, Rhode Island; Manchester, Exeter, Concord, and Dover, New Hampshire; and Hartford, New Haven, Bridgeport, Norwich, and Meriden, Connecticut. In the midst of that whirlwind tour, he complained to his wife: "I have been unable to escape this toil. If I had foreseen it, I think I would not have come East at all. The speech at New York, being within my calculation before I started, went off passably well and gave me no trouble whatever. The difficulty was to make nine others, before reading audiences who have already seen all my ideas in print."

Robert Todd Lincoln, the eldest son of the future President, hoped to attend Harvard University, but in 1859 he failed the entrance exams. So he entered Phillips Exeter Academy, a college prep school in Exeter, New Hampshire, that had opened in 1783. The founder was John Phillips, the uncle of Samuel Phillips Jr., who had established Phillips Academy at Andover, Massachusetts, five years earlier. Among other famous Exeter alumni were Daniel Webster, whom Lincoln admired greatly, and Franklin Pierce, whom Lincoln ridiculed during the 1852 presidential campaign. U. S. Grant also sent his son (U. S. Grant Jr.) to Exeter. Robert entered Harvard in 1860.

ABRAHAM LINCOLN ATTENDED SERVICES WITH HIS SON ROBERT AT THE SECOND PARISH CONGREGATIONAL CHURCH WHILE VISITING EXETER, NEW HAMPSHIRE. THE PEW USED BY LINCOLN IS NOW IN THE NEARBY EXETER CONGREGATIONAL CHURCH LOCATED ON FRONT STREET.

THE COOPER INSTITUTE AND NEW ENGLAND

Saturday I came back to Exeter, reaching here about noon, and finding the boys all right, having caught up with their lessons.

LETTER TO MARY TODD LINCOLN, MARCH 4, 1860

In Exeter, Lincoln also impressed his audience, which consisted of many highly educated townspeople, as well as Lincoln's son, Robert, and his schoolmates. During Lincoln's presentation he threw out questions; upon receiving no answers, he remarked: "You people here don't jaw back at a fellow as they do out West." Despite his unfamiliar style, Lincoln captured his auditors, even those who had found his appearance uncouth and Western expressions peculiar. When Lincoln first took the stage, one boy whispered, "Don't you feel kind of sorry for Bob?" A girl remarked, "Isn't it too bad Bob's got such a homely father?" But after his speech, the students no longer pitied Robert; they took pride in his father. Robert accompanied his father on his next stops at Concord, Manchester, and Dover, where he continued to enjoy success.

ABOVE: ABRAHAM LINCOLN VISITED HIS SON ROBERT AT THE FOLSOM BLOCK BOARDING HOUSE WHERE ROBERT LIVED WHILE ATTENDING PHILLIPS EXETER ACADEMY IN EXETER, NEW HAMPSHIRE.

FOLLOWING PAGE: LINCOLN GAVE A SPEECH AT THE EXETER TOWN HALL TO A LARGE CROWD. THE TOWN HALL HAS CHANGED VERY LITTLE AND IS STILL ACTIVELY USED BY THE COMMUNITY.

ELECTED SIXTEENTH PRESIDENT OF THE UNITED STATES

... that very great responsibility rests upon me in the position to which the votes of the American people have called me. I am deeply sensible of that weighty responsibility.

ADDRESS TO THE OHIO LEGISLATURE, COLUMBUS, FEBRUARY 13, 1861

In the Illinois state capitol, Lincoln occupied the governor's office, which that official used only while the legislature was in session. Measuring approximately fifteen by twelve feet, and furnished with a sofa, a table, and a few armchairs, it could accommodate up to a dozen people comfortably. On a desk where his secretary worked were "countless letters and files of newspapers, and quite an assortment of odd presents." Lincoln received hundreds of gifts and souvenirs, including canes, axes, mauls, fragments of old rails that he had allegedly split and of the cabins where he had supposedly lived, pieces of furniture and surveyor's tools he had once owned, mementos of the Black Hawk War, wedges, pictures, books, and a chain of links ingeniously carved from a single piece of wood.

ABRAHAM LINCOLN USED THE GOVERNOR'S ROOM IN THE OLD STATE CAPITOL IN SPRINGFIELD FOR HIS PRESIDENTIAL CAMPAIGN HEADQUARTERS AND FOR HIS OFFICE OF PRESIDENT-ELECT AFTER BEING ELECTED PRESIDENT. THANKS TO A DETAILED ILLUSTRATION MADE IN 1860, THE ROOM APPEARS AS IT DID WHEN IT WAS LINCOLN'S OFFICE. (NATIONAL HISTORIC LANDMARK)

Newspaper editors sent innumerable copies of their journals, all carefully marked up for the inspection of the President-elect, who did not read them. In time, the governor's office came to resemble "a museum of curiosities." The various tools provided Lincoln "an opportunity to entertain even his polished city-bred callers with explanations and anecdotes about the use or importance of these, to them, unfamiliar implements." A well-wisher who observed two steel wedges asked: "Are those the wedges, Sir?" Lincoln replied: "These, Sir, are the identical wedges – that were sent to me about a week ago."

At the governor's office, Lincoln "made himself the Mecca to which all politicians made pilgrimages. He told them all a story, said nothing, and sent them away." Uncomplainingly he met not only politicos but ordinary people. "I am a public man now," he said, "and I am the public's most obedient servant." An observer sketched his method of dealing with callers: "Possessed of an unparalleled equanimity of temperament, and yet endowed with an iron-like firmness, he lends a willing ear to every visitor, patiently hears them through, and in every case dismisses them with a dignity and an affability that inspires the loftiest respect and admiration of his character. In no case have I heard of any man coming out of Mr. Lincoln's presence with feelings other than those of admiration and satisfaction." Among the more noteworthy interviews were those "with extreme Southern gentlemen, who come full of prejudices against him but who left, satisfied with his loyalty to all the constitutional rights of the South."

LEFT: THIS PORTRAIT OF ABRAHAM LINCOLN WAS MADE BY PRESTON BUTLER IN SPRINGFIELD ON AUGUST 13, 1860, SHORTLY AFTER LINCOLN RECEIVED THE NOMINATION FOR PRESIDENT.

RIGHT: LINCOLN'S PRESIDENTIAL CAMPAIGN HEADQUARTERS AND HIS OFFICE OF PRESIDENT-ELECT WERE IN THE SOUTHEAST CORNER OF THE OLD STATE CAPITOL STATE HISTORIC SITE IN SPRINGFIELD, ILLINOIS.

ELECTED SIXTEENTH PRESIDENT OF THE UNITED STATES

...I prefer a very great crowd should not gather at Chicago.

LETTER TO JOSHUA SPEED, NOVEMBER 19, 1860

ABRAHAM LINCOLN MADE HIS LAST PUBLIC APPEARANCE IN CHICAGO WHILE ATTENDING SERVICES AT ST. JAMES CHURCH (NOW THE ST. JAMES CATHEDRAL). DUE TO THE GREAT CHICAGO FIRE OF 1871, THE STONE CHURCH IS ALSO THE ONLY SURVIVING BUILDING IN CHICAGO WHICH LINCOLN VISITED.

Springfield. Ills. Nov. 19. 1860

Dear Speed

Yours of the 14th. is received. I shall be at Chicago Thursday the 22nd. Inst. and one or two succeeding days. Could you not meet me there? Mary thinks of going with me; and therefore I suggest that Mrs. S. accompany you. Please let this be private, as I prefer a very great crowd should not gather at Chicago. Respects to Mrs. S.　　Your friend, as ever A. Lincoln

LETTER TO JOSHUA SPEED, THIRTEEN DAYS AFTER BEING ELECTED PRESIDENT, NOVEMBER 19, 1860

I have always hated slavery, I think as much as any Abolitionist. [APPLAUSE] I have been an Old Line Whig. I have always hated it, but I have always been quiet about it until this new era of the introduction of the Nebraska Bill began. I always believed that everybody was against it, and that it was in course of ultimate extinction. [POINTING TO MR. BROWNING WHO STOOD NEAR BY] Browning thought so; the great mass of the nation have rested in the belief that slavery was in course of ultimate extinction. They had reason so to believe.

SPEECH AT CHICAGO, JULY 10, 1858

In late November Lincoln conferred at Chicago with Vice-President-elect Hannibal Hamlin about Cabinet appointments. Lincoln did not enjoy his visit to the city, for the "aristocratic noodles of the Michigan avenue" had ridiculed "the plain republican habits of the President and his lady." Back in Springfield, he complained about the social whirl he had endured in the metropolis; a journalist reported that his "sketch of the dinner and other parties, and the Sunday school meetings he had to attend – of the crowds of [the] curious that importuned him at all hours of the day, of the public levees he was obliged to hold, &c., &c., was graphic. It seems that instead of enjoying rest and relief, as expected, he was even more molested than in this place. If people only knew his holy horror of public ovations, they would probably treat him more sparingly. To be lugged around from place to place to satisfy the curiosity of the populace, is a doubtful mode of bestowing honor and rendering homage."

PRESIDENT-ELECT ABRAHAM LINCOLN WENT TO CHICAGO TO MEET WITH VICE-PRESIDENT-ELECT HANNIBAL HAMLIN AND OTHERS CONCERNING THE ESTABLISHMENT OF HIS CABINET.

Leaving Springfield, Illinois

Here I have lived a quarter of a century, and have passed from a young to an old man. Here my children have been born, and one is buried.

Farewell Address, Springfield, February 11, 1861

President-elect Abraham and Mary Lincoln attended a gala reception in this house the night before Lincoln left for Washington, D.C. The Lincolns had attended social gatherings here while living in Springfield. It later became the home of noted poet Vachel Lindsay, Vachel Lindsay State Historic Site, Springfield, Illinois. (National Historic Landmark)

Springfield, Ills. Oct 19. 1860

Miss Grace Bedell
My dear little Miss.

Your very agreeable letter of the 15th. is received.

I regret the necessity of saying I have no daughters. I have three sons—one seventeen, one nine, and one seven, years of age. They, with their mother, constitute my whole family.

As to the whiskers, having never worn any, do you not think people would call it a piece of silly affection if I were to begin it now?
Your very sincere well-wisher A. Lincoln

LETTER TO GRACE BEDELL, LITTLE GIRL IN WESTFIELD, NEW YORK, OCTOBER 19, 1860

In the 1850s, Lincoln's brother-in-law, the Springfield merchant Clark M. Smith, owned this 1846 Greek Revival home, which the parents of poet Vachel Lindsay (author of "Abraham Lincoln Walks at Midnight") acquired after the Civil War. Smith and his wife, nee Ann Marie Todd, entertained the Lincolns here. Mary Todd Lincoln called her sister a woman who "possesses such a miserable disposition & so false a tongue" that "no one respects" her. Ann's "tongue for so many years, has been considered 'no slander' – and as a child & young girl, [she] could not be outdone in falsehood. . . . I grieve for those, who have to come in contact with her malice, yet even that, is so well understood, [that] the object of her wrath, generally rises, with good people, in proportion to her vindictiveness." (When shown this assessment of her character, Ann replied with some justice: "Mary was writing about herself.")

A REPLICA OF A PARADE FLOAT USED IN A LINCOLN PRESIDENTIAL RALLY, LINCOLN HOME NATIONAL HISTORIC SITE, SPRINGFIELD.
(NATIONAL HISTORIC LANDMARK)

She proved a good and kind mother to A. and is still living in Coles Co. Illinois.

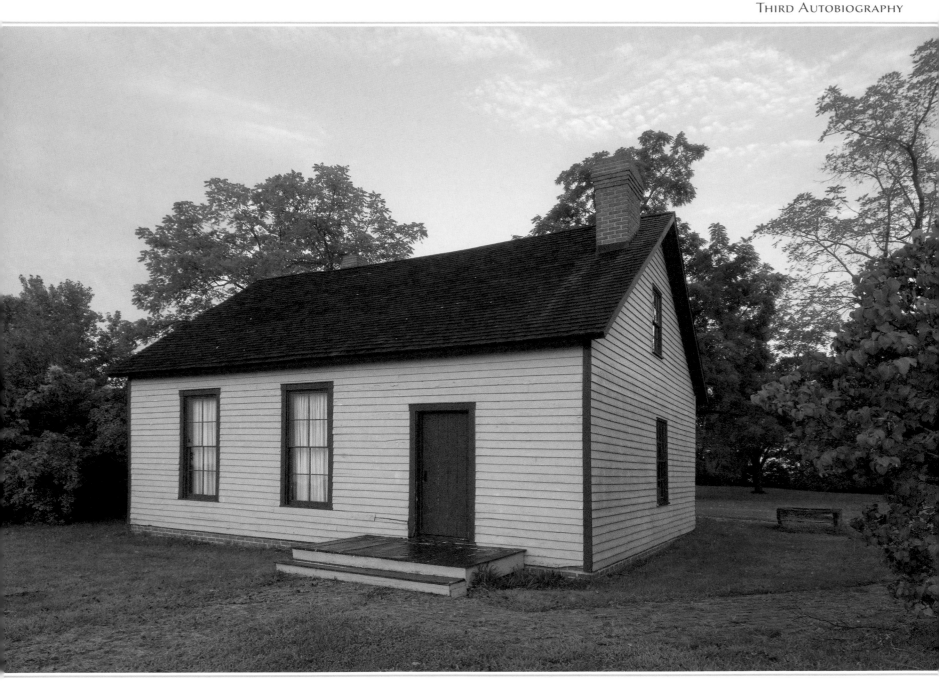

Dear John

I now think I will pass Decatur, going to Coles, on the day after to-morrow — Wednesday, the 30th. of the month. Be ready, and go along.

Yours as ever A. Lincoln

Letter to cousin John Hanks soon before Lincoln's last visit to his stepmother Sarah, January 28, 1861

The Rueben Moore Home, where Abraham Lincoln visited his stepmother Sarah Bush Lincoln prior to going to Washington, D.C., is now part of Lincoln Log Cabin State Historic Site south of Charleston, Illinois.

Dear Brother

Your proposal about selling the East forty acres of land is all that I want or could claim for myself; but I am not satisfied with it on Mother's account. I want her to have her living, and I feel that it is my duty, to some extent, to see that she is not wronged. She had a right of Dower (that is, the use of one third for life) in the other two forties; but, it seems, she has already let you take that, hook and line. She now has the use of the whole of the East forty, as long as she lives; and if it be sold, of course, she is intitled to the interest on all the money it brings, as long as she lives; but you propose to sell it for three hundred dollars, take one hundred away with you, and leave her two hundred, at 8 per cent, making her the enormous sum of 16 dollars a year. Now, if you are satisfied with treating her in that way, I am not.

LETTER TO STEPBROTHER JOHN D. JOHNSTON, NOVEMBER 25, 1851

In taking leave of Sarah Bush Lincoln, whom he saw at Farmington near Charleston on January 30, Lincoln "was very affectionate." She was living with Augustus H. Chapman, who asked Lincoln to visit her: "She is getting somewhat childish and is very uneasy about you fearing some of your political opponents will kill you. She is very anxious to see you once more." In their biography of Lincoln, William Herndon and Jesse Weik described the scene: "The separation from his step-mother was particularly touching. Lincoln's love for his second mother was a most filial and affectionate one. The parting, when the good old woman, with tears streaming down her cheeks, gave him a mother's benediction, expressing the fear that his life might be taken by his enemies, will never be forgotten by those who witnessed it. Deeply impressed by this farewell scene Mr. Lincoln reluctantly withdrew from the circle of warm friends who crowded around him, and, filled with gloomy forebodings of the future, returned to Springfield."

SUNRISE AT THE RUEBEN MOORE HOME, PART OF THE FARMINGTON SETTLEMENT,
ONE MILE NORTH OF LINCOLN LOG CABIN STATE HISTORIC SITE NEAR LERNA, ILLINOIS.

Leaving Springfield, Illinois

My friends—no one, not in my situation, can appreciate my feeling of sadness at this parting. To this place, and the kindness of these people, I owe everything.

FAREWELL ADDRESS, SPRINGFIELD, FEBRUARY 11, 1861

AFTER ABRAHAM LINCOLN WAS ELECTED PRESIDENT, HE BECAME INUNDATED WITH LETTERS, REQUESTS, AND PREPARATIONS, EVEN BEFORE HE LEFT SPRINGFIELD, LINCOLN HOME NATIONAL HISTORIC SITE. (NATIONAL HISTORIC LANDMARK)

By late January 1861, Lincoln was devoting much time to his inaugural address and to the speeches he would deliver en route to Washington. To concentrate on that task and avoid distracting visits, he squirreled himself away in a small, little-used room of the store owned by his brother-in-law, Clark M. Smith, who provided a table and chair, the only furniture available to Lincoln there. He also took refuge in the hotel room of Thomas D. Jones, a Cincinnati sculptor who was executing a bust of the President-elect. William Herndon recalled that in late January, Lincoln "informed me that he was ready to begin the preparation of his inaugural address. He had, aside from his law books and the few gilded volumes that ornamented the centre-table in his parlor at home, comparatively no library. He never seemed to care to own or collect books. On the other hand I had a very respectable collection, and was adding to it every day. To my library Lincoln very frequently had access. When, therefore, he began on his inaugural speech he told me what works he intended to consult. I looked for a long list, but when he went over it I was greatly surprised. He asked me to furnish him with Henry Clay's great speech delivered in 1850; Andrew Jackson's proclamation against Nullification; and a copy of the Constitution. He afterwards called for Webster's reply to Hayne, a speech which he read when he lived at New Salem, and which he always regarded as the grandest specimen of American oratory." Herndon also supplied a copy of George Washington's farewell address. With these few books and documents at his fingertips, Lincoln secluded himself at Smith's store and drafted his inaugural.

LINCOLN WROTE LETTERS AND LIKELY WORKED ON SPEECHES AT THIS DESK IN HIS HOME. BEFORE LEAVING SPRINGFIELD, HE BEGAN WRITING HIS FIRST INAUGURAL ADDRESS AND WROTE HIS FAREWELL ADDRESS, LINCOLN HOME NATIONAL HISTORIC SITE.

Leaving Springfield, Illinois

I now leave, not knowing when, or whether ever, I may return . . .

FAREWELL ADDRESS, SPRINGFIELD, FEBRUARY 11, 1861

On the morning of February 11, Lincoln spent half an hour at the small, dingy depot shaking hands with innumerable friends and neighbors. As he did so, he was deeply moved and could hardly speak. The mood was solemn and anxious as he mounted the platform of the train's rear car. There, a friend noted, his "breast heaved with emotion and he could scarcely command his feelings sufficiently to commence." For a few seconds he surveyed the crowd of a thousand well-wishers, Republicans and Democrats alike, as the cold wind blew a combination of snow and rain into their faces. Only the locomotive's steady hissing broke the silence.

ABOVE: THE LAST LIGHT OF THE DAY SETS OVER ABRAHAM LINCOLN'S HOME IN SPRINGFIELD, ILLINOIS.
(NATIONAL HISTORIC LANDMARK)

FOLLOWING PAGE: LINCOLN LEFT SPRINGFIELD FOR WASHINGTON, D.C. BY TRAIN AT THE GREAT WESTERN RAILROAD DEPOT IN SPRINGFIELD, ILLINOIS, WHERE HE MADE HIS FAREWELL ADDRESS TO FRIENDS AND THE PEOPLE OF SPRINGFIELD.

My friends.

No one, not in my situation, can appreciate my feeling of sadness at this parting. To this place, and the kindness of these people, I owe every thing. Here I have lived a quarter of a century, and have passed from a young to an old man. Here my children have been born, and one is buried. I now leave, not knowing when, or whether ever, I may return, with a task before me greater than that which rested upon Washington. Without the assistance of that Divine Being, who ever attended him, I cannot succeed. With that assistance I cannot fail. Trusting in Him, who can go with me, and remain with you and be every where for good, let us confidently hope that all will yet be well. To His care commending you, as I hope in your prayers you will commend me, I bid you an affectionate farewell.

FAREWELL ADDRESS FROM GREAT WESTERN RAILROAD DEPOT, SPRINGFIELD, FEBRUARY 11, 1861

FIFTY MONTHS AS PRESIDENT

. . . the Union of these States is perpetual. FIRST INAUGURAL ADDRESS, MARCH 4, 1861

ABRAHAM LINCOLN'S FIRST AND SECOND INAUGURATIONS TOOK PLACE ON THE EAST SIDE OF THE UNITED STATES CAPITOL
IN WASHINGTON, D.C., WHERE HE HAD SERVED AS A REPRESENTATIVE OF ILLINOIS IN THE 30TH CONGRESS TWELVE YEARS BEFORE.
INAUGURATIONS IN PRESENT TIMES TAKE PLACE ON THE WEST SIDE OF THE CAPITOL.
(NATIONAL HISTORIC LANDMARK)

In your hands, my dissatisfied fellow countrymen, and not in mine, is the momentous issue of civil war. The government will not assail you. You can have no conflict, without being yourselves the aggressors. You have no oath registered in Heaven to destroy the government, while I shall have the most solemn one to "preserve, protect and defend" it. . . . We are not enemies, but friends. We must not be enemies. Though passion may have strained, it must not break our bonds of affection. The mystic chords of memory, streching from every battle-field, and patriot grave, to every living heart and hearthstone, all over this broad land, will yet swell the chorus of the Union, when again touched, as surely they will be, by the better angels of our nature.

First Inaugural Address, March 4, 1861

At dawn on March 4, crowds began gathering at the Capitol. Two thousand volunteer soldiers, organized by Colonel Charles P. Stone acting on General Winfield Scott's orders, deployed to their posts; 653 regular troops, summoned from distant forts, together with the marines based at the navy yard, supplemented their ranks. Sharpshooters clambered to the roofs of the taller buildings flanking Pennsylvania Avenue, along which police took up positions. Cavalry patrolled the side streets. Plainclothes detectives circulated among the crowd with instructions to arrest for "disorderly conduct" anyone speaking disrespectfully of the new President. The sound of fife and drum filled the air. Flags and banners fluttered in the chill wind. Rumors of bloody doings were bruited about, though the heavy military presence made it unlikely that anyone would disturb the day's ceremony. Colorfully-attired marshals assembled, ready to lead the procession. Gradually the streets became choked with humanity, eagerly awaiting the appearance of the President-elect. Good humor, decorum, order, and enthusiasm prevailed among the people who turned out to witness the event, which took place on a temporary platform that was erected over the steps of the east portico of the Capitol. Above it loomed the skeletal, half-finished, new cast-iron dome; before it stood thousands of cheering spectators of all ages and both sexes, coming from near and far. As Lincoln was about to speak, the clouds which had seemed so threatening that morning lifted, giving way to cheerful, bright sunshine.

Fifty Months as President

Nowhere in the world is presented a government of so much liberty and equality. To the humblest and poorest amongst us are held out the highest privileges and positions. The present moment finds me at the White House, yet there is as good a chance for your children as there was for my father's.

Speech to One Hundred Forty-eighth Ohio Regiment, August 31, 1864

The White House was officially named the Executive Mansion when Abraham Lincoln was President.
View from Pennsylvania Avenue near the end of a spring day in Washington, D.C.
(National Historic Landmark)

It is not merely for to-day, but for all time to come that we should perpetuate for our children's children this great and free government, which we have enjoyed all our lives. I beg you to remember this, not merely for my sake, but for yours. I happen temporarily to occupy this big White House. I am a living witness that any one of your children may look to come here as my father's child has.

SPEECH TO ONE HUNDRED SIXTY-SIXTH OHIO REGIMENT, AUGUST 22, 1864

THE SOUTH LAWN OF THE WHITE HOUSE NEAR THE END OF AN AUTUMN DAY IN WASHINGTON, D.C.
SOON AFTER THE ATTACK ON FT. SUMTER, UNION BATTALIONS FILLED THE SOUTH LAWN WHILE GUARDING THE WHITE HOUSE.
COLONEL ELMER ELLSWORTH'S ZOUAVE REGIMENT SET UP CAMP ON THE LAWN OF THE WHITE HOUSE AND CALLED IT "CAMP LINCOLN."
SOME TROOPS EVEN CAMPED OUT IN THE EAST ROOM FOR A SHORT TIME, THE LARGEST ROOM IN THE HOUSE.

Four Years of Civil War

My paramount object in this struggle is to save the Union . . . I have here stated my purpose according to my view of official duty; and I intend no modification of my oft-expressed personal wish that all men every where could be free.

Yours, A. Lincoln

LETTER TO HORACE GREELEY, AUGUST 22, 1862

THE SMITHSONIAN CASTLE IS THE ORIGINAL SMITHSONIAN BUILDING LOCATED ON THE NATIONAL MALL IN WASHINGTON, D.C.
PRESIDENT LINCOLN ATTENDED A LECTURE AND HANDED OUT AWARDS AT A SCHOOL PROGRAM AT THE SMITHSONIAN CASTLE.
(NATIONAL HISTORIC LANDMARK)

My dear Sir

Your very kind letter of the 16th. to Mr. Colfax, has been shown me by him. I am grateful for the generous sentiments and purposes expressed towards the administration. Of course I am anxious to see the policy proposed in the late special message, go forward; but you have advocated it from the first, so that I need to say little to you on the subject. If I were to suggest anything it would be that as the North are already for the measure, we should urge it persuasively, and not menacingly, upon the South. I am a little uneasy about the abolishment of slavery in this District, not but I would be glad to see it abolished, but as to the time and manner of doing it.

LETTER TO HORACE GREELEY, MARCH 24, 1862

In 1861 and 1862, the Smithsonian Institution hosted an anti-slavery lecture series. When told that Horace Greeley, editor of the New York Tribune and the nation's most influential journalist, was to deliver a lecture there, Lincoln said: "I never heard Greeley, and I want to hear him. In print every one of his words seems to weigh about a ton; I want to see what he has to say about us." In the midst of the lecture, Greeley looked at the President as he insisted that abolition of slavery was the "sole purpose of the war." Antislavery Congressman George W. Julian of Indiana wrote that Mr. Lincoln "greatly admired" the lecture: "I sat by his side, and at the conclusion of the discourse he said to me: 'That address is full of good thoughts, and I would like to take the manuscript home with me and carefully read it over.'"

THIS REFLECTIVE PORTRAIT OF ABRAHAM LINCOLN WAS MADE BY AN UNKNOWN PHOTOGRAPHER
AT THE MATHEW BRADY GALLERY ON MAY 16, 1861, IN WASHINGTON, D.C., TWO DAYS BEFORE
LINCOLN TRAVELED TO THE GREAT FALLS AND BEHIND CONFEDERATE LINES INSPECTING UNION DEFENSES.

But suppose Virginia sends her troops, or admits others through her borders, to assail this capital, am I not to repel them, even to the crossing of the Potomac if I can? Suppose Virginia erects, or permits to be erected, batteries on the opposite shore, to bombard the city, are we to stand still and see it done? In a word, if Virginia strikes us, are we not to strike back, and as effectively as we can?

LETTER TO REVERDY JOHNSON, APRIL 24, 1861

You will please to have as strong a War Steamer as you can conveniently put on that duty, to cruise upon the Potomac, and to look in upon, and, if practicable, examine the Bluff and vicinity, at what is called the White House, once or twice per day; and, in case of any attempt to erect a battery there, to drive away the party attempting it, if practicable; and, in every event to report daily to your Department, and to me.

LETTER TO SECRETARY OF THE NAVY GIDEON WELLES, APRIL 29, 1861

The defeat at Bull Run in July 1861 profoundly affected Lincoln, who with "intense feeling" remarked, "if Hell is [not any worse than this, it has no terror for me." But he did not wallow in self-pity or pessimistic gloom. The morning after the battle, he said: "There is nothing in this except the lives lost and the lives which must be lost to make it good." Lincoln assured House Speaker Galusha Grow: "My boys are green at the fighting business," but "wait till they get licked enough to raise their dander! Then the cry will be, 'On to Richmond' and 'no Stone-walls will stop them!'" In early August he told a despondent friend: "We were all too confident – too sure of an easy victory. We now understand the difficulties in the way, and shall surmount them." Years later, Walt Whitman paid tribute to Lincoln's resilience: "If there were nothing else of Abraham Lincoln for history to stamp him with, it is enough to send him with his wreath to the memory of all future time, that he endured that hour, that day, bitterer than gall – indeed a crucifixion day – that it did not conquer him – that he unflinchingly stemm'd it, and resolv'd to lift himself and the Union out of it."

ABOVE: THE LAST LIGHT OF AN AUTUMN DAY ON THE GREAT FALLS OF THE POTOMAC RIVER, VIRGINIA.
PRESIDENT LINCOLN VISITED THE GREAT FALLS TWO DAYS IN A ROW WHILE INSPECTING THE BANKS OF THE RIVER,
THE FIRST DAY PASSING CONFEDERATE PICKETS IN VIRGINIA TWICE WITHOUT BEING RECOGNIZED. THE SECOND DAY,
PRESIDENT LINCOLN TRAVELED WITH SECRETARY OF STATE WILLIAM SEWARD AND GENERAL MONTGOMERY MEIGS.

PREVIOUS PAGE: MATHER GORGE RUNS DOWNSTREAM FROM THE GREAT FALLS OF THE POTOMAC RIVER
AT GREAT FALLS PARK OPERATED BY THE NATIONAL PARK SERVICE, VIRGINIA.
MARYLAND IS ON THE RIGHT (NORTH) BANK AND VIRGINIA IS ON THE LEFT (SOUTH).

Four Years of Civil War

...after the late battles at and near Bull Run, an expedition went out from Washington under a flag of truce to bury the dead and bring in the wounded, and the rebels seized the blacks who went along to help and sent them into slavery...

Reply to Emancipation Memorial presented by Chicago Christians of all denominations, September 13, 1862

A large anvil top storm over Washington, D.C. can be seen from Manassas National Battlefield Park, Virginia.
The First Battle of Manassas, or Bull Run, was the first large battle of the Civil War.
Cannons in the battle were distinctly heard in Washington, D.C., twenty-five miles away.

I have always thought that all men should be free; but if any should be slaves it should be first those who desire it for themselves, and secondly those who desire it for others. Whenever I hear any one, arguing for slavery I feel a strong impulse to see it tried on him personally.   SPEECH TO ONE HUNDRED FORTIETH INDIANA REGIMENT, MARCH 17, 1865

A SUMMER SUNSET ON THE POTOMAC RIVER AT THE BASE OF THE RIVER BLUFF AT TURKEY RUN PARK, VIRGINIA.
THIS LOCATION ON THE POTOMAC RIVER IS EIGHT MILES FROM THE WHITE HOUSE.

And, once more let me tell you, it is indispensable to you that you strike a blow. . . . But you must act.

DISPATCH TO GENERAL GEORGE McCLELLAN, APRIL 9, 1862

Your despatches complaining that you are not properly sustained, while they do not offend me, do pain me very much. . . . And, once more let me tell you, it is indispensable to you that you strike a blow. I am powerless to help this. . . . The country will not fail to note—is now noting—that the present hesitation to move upon an intrenched enemy, is but the story of Manassas repeated. I beg to assure you that I have never written you, or spoken to you, in greater kindness of feeling than now, nor with a fuller purpose to sustain you, so far as in my most anxious judgment, I consistently can. But you must act.

DISPATCH TO GENERAL GEORGE McCLELLAN, APRIL 9, 1862

On May 22-23, 1862, Lincoln visited General Irvin McDowell's corps at Fredericksburg. Since it had been decided to forward McDowell's troops to General George McClellan, who was leading the Army of the Potomac against Richmond, the President wanted to expedite that transfer. While proceeding from the landing at Aquia Creek to the general's headquarters at Chatham Manor, built in the 1770s, he admired a new railroad bridge across Potomac Creek, an immense structure 400 feet long and 100 feet high, which, he said wonderingly, contained nothing but "beanpoles and cornstalks." He reviewed the troops and consulted their commander, who declared he could be ready to march south on Sunday, May 25. But Lincoln suggested that he "take a good ready" and start out on Monday. While inspecting the troops, he was within view of Confederates across the river who could have shot him. Commented one journalist, "Mr. Lincoln is certainly devoid of personal timidity."

ABOVE: PRESIDENT LINCOLN HAD A MEETING WITH GENERAL IRVIN McDOWELL AT CHATHAM MANOR SEVEN MONTHS BEFORE THE BATTLE OF FREDERICKSBURG, FREDERICKSBURG NATIONAL MILITARY PARK, VIRGINIA.

PREVIOUS LEFT: THE SHADOW OF THE TWO CATALPA TREES ON THE HOUSE AT CHATHAM MANOR, BELIEVED TO BE THE TREES WRITTEN ABOUT BY WALT WHITMAN WHILE HE SERVED AS A FIELD HOSPITAL NURSE AFTER THE BATTLE OF FREDERICKSBURG.

PREVIOUS RIGHT: THE VIEW OF THE RAPPAHANNOCK RIVER AND FREDERICKSBURG FROM CHATHAM MANOR, FREDERICKSBURG NATIONAL MILITARY PARK, VIRGINIA.

I expect to maintain this contest until successful, or till I die, or am conquered, or my term expires, or Congress or the country forsakes me;

LETTER TO SECRETARY OF STATE WILLIAM H. SEWARD, JUNE 28, 1862

THE SOUTH SIDE OF PRESIDENT LINCOLN'S COTTAGE AT THE SOLDIERS' HOME NATIONAL MONUMENT IN WASHINGTON, D.C., WHERE THE LINCOLNS RESIDED FROM JUNE TO NOVEMBER OF 1862, 1863, AND 1864 TO ESCAPE THE SUMMER HEAT AND TO BUFFER THE POLITICAL PRESSURE OF THE WHITE HOUSE. (NATIONAL HISTORIC LANDMARK)

. . . by His divine law, nations like individuals are subjected to punishments and chastisements in this world, may we not justly fear that the awful calamity of civil war, which now desolates the land, may be but a punishment, inflicted upon us, for our presumptuous sins, to the needful end of our national reformation as a whole People? We have been the recipients of the choicest bounties of Heaven. We have been preserved, these many years, in peace and prosperity. We have grown in numbers, wealth and power, as no other nation has ever grown. But we have forgotten God. We have forgotten the gracious hand which preserved us in peace, and multiplied and enriched and strengthened us; and we have vainly imagined, in the deceitfulness of our hearts, that all these blessings were produced by some superior wisdom and virtue of our own. Intoxicated with unbroken success, we have become too self-sufficient to feel the necessity of redeeming and preserving grace, too proud to pray to the God that made us!

PROCLAMATION APPOINTING A NATIONAL FAST DAY, MARCH 30, 1863

Lincoln and his family spent the warmer months of 1862, 1863, and 1864 at the Soldiers' Home, a complex of five buildings on 300 acres, located three miles north of The White House. Established in the early 1850s as a retreat for indigent, disabled veterans, it was officially known as the Military Asylum. On its grounds, the wealthy banker George W. Riggs built a comfortable house in the Rural Gothic style, which in time became known as the Anderson Cottage. This dwelling is in all likelihood the one in which the Lincolns stayed. "We are truly delighted with this retreat, the drives & walks around here are truly delightful," Mary Lincoln wrote. The Soldiers' Home occupied high ground, catching whatever breezes might be blowing in the area and offering a splendid view of Washington.

THE FRONT OF PRESIDENT LINCOLN'S COTTAGE AT THE SOLDIERS' HOME NATIONAL MONUMENT. ABRAHAM LINCOLN COMPLETED DRAFTS OF THE PRELIMINARY EMANCIPATION PROCLAMATION AT THE SOLDIERS' HOME.

Four Years of Civil War

A circle whose circumference shall pass through Harper's Ferry, Front-Royal, and Strasburg, and whose center shall be a little North East of Winchester, almost certainly has within it this morning, the forces of Jackson, Ewell, and Edward Johnson. Quite certainly they were within it two days ago. Some part of these forces attacked Harper's Ferry at dark last evening, and are still in sight this morning.

Dispatch to General George McClellan, May 31, 1862

View from the Maryland bank as fog hangs in the Virginia Blue Ridge around the Potomac River, Harpers Ferry National Historical Park. President Lincoln stayed at Harpers Ferry, meeting with his generals and reviewing troops at several locations.

On September 15, 1862, Confederate forces captured the 11,500-man Union garrison at Harper's Ferry. Lincoln deplored this calamity, saying that General George McClellan "could and ought to have prevented the loss of Harper's Ferry, but was six days marching 40 miles, and it was surrendered." Two weeks later, after the epic Battle of Antietam, Lincoln visited the army and reviewed troops at Boliver Heights, overlooking Harper's Ferry. As he passed the crimson-clad Fifth New York Zouaves, which had suffered heavy losses, he stopped and remarked to a general: "And these are the red legged devils. I know from the reports that there has been no such thing as beating them, even round a stump." Turning to the troops, he said: "Boys, your thinned ranks and shattered flags tell the story of your bravery. The people thank you and so do I." At General Brooks Morell's division he paused again. "Those flags are more tattered now than when I saw them at Harrison's Landing," he told the general; "the regiments have reason to be proud of such flags, and you of such men." He was dismayed to see how small some regiments had become since he last visited the army. "I thought they were merely a corporal's guard," he said in astonishment.

TOP LEFT: FOG LIFTS AT SUNRISE OVER THE POTOMAC RIVER. VIEW FROM THE MARYLAND BANK LOOKING TO THE BLUE RIDGE OF VIRGINIA ON THE FAR BANK.

TOP RIGHT: THE SHENANDOAH RIVER FLOWING TO THE CONFLUENCE WITH THE POTOMAC RIVER. VIEW FROM THE WEST VIRGINIA BANK LOOKING TO THE BLUE RIDGE OF VIRGINIA.

BOTTOM: JOHN BROWN'S FORT IS THE ONLY ARMORY BUILDING TO ESCAPE DESTRUCTION DURING THE CIVIL WAR, HARPERS FERRY NATIONAL HISTORICAL PARK, WEST VIRGINIA.

Your despatches of to-day received. God bless you, and all with you. Destroy the rebel army, if possible. DISPATCH TO GENERAL GEORGE MCCLELLAN, SEPTEMBER 15, 1862

Since telegraphing you, despatch came from Gen. McClellan, dated, 7 o'clock this morning. Nothing of importance happened with him yesterday. This morning he was up with the enemy at Sharpsburg, and was waiting for heavy fog to rise.

TELEGRAM TO ANDREW G. CURTIN, SEPTEMBER 16, 1862

THIS PHOTOGRAPH OF ABRAHAM LINCOLN WAS MADE BY ALEXANDER GARDNER ON OCTOBER 3, 1862, AT THE HEADQUARTERS OF GENERAL FITZ JOHN PORTER, TWO WEEKS AFTER THE SEPTEMBER 17 BATTLE OF ANTIETAM. PRESIDENT LINCOLN CAME TO MEET WITH GENERAL GEORGE MCCLELLAN AND REVIEW THE ARMY OF THE POTOMAC.

Governor Curtin telegraphs me:

"I have advices that Jackson is crossing the Potomac at Williamsport, and probably the whole rebel army will be drawn from Maryland."

Receiving nothing from Harper's Ferry or Martinsburg to-day, and positive information from Wheeling that the line is cut, corroborates the idea that the enemy is recrossing the Potomac. Please do not let him get off without being hurt.

DISPATCH TO GENERAL GEORGE McCLELLAN, SEPTEMBER 12—5:45 P.M., 1862

In early October 1862, two weeks after the bloody Union semi-victory at the Battle of Antietam, Lincoln visited the Army of the Potomac "to satisfy himself personally, without the intervention of anybody, of the purposes, intentions, and fidelity of [General George B.] McClellan, his officers, and the army." During his three days with the army in Maryland, Lincoln visited hospitals, inspected the troops, and conferred with McClellan. The soldiers were pleased to have the President in their midst. A sergeant from Massachusetts reported that he "could easily perceive why and how he was called 'Honest Abe.' . . . I think his coming down, or up, to see us done us all good." Lincoln instructed the troops' commander, General McClellan, to launch an advance within two weeks. He was dismayed that McClellan seemed unwilling to have them pursue Lee after the Battle of Antietam. One evening, the President asked a friend as they stood on a hill and surveyed the vast army encampment:

"What do you suppose all these people are?"

"Why, I suppose it to be a part of the grand army."

Lincoln, "in a tone of patient but melancholy sarcasm," corrected him: "No, you are mistaken.

That is General McClellan's body guard."

THE PHOTOGRAPH AT LEFT OF PRESIDENT LINCOLN AND HIS GENERALS WAS MADE AT WHAT WAS THEN
THE STEPHEN GROVE HOME AND FARM, WHICH CAN BE SEEN IN THE BACK OF THE PHOTOGRAPH.
NOW A PRIVATE RESIDENCE, THE HOUSE STILL STANDS AND IS LOCATED IN THE TREES, UPPER LEFT
IN THE PHOTOGRAPH ABOVE. LINCOLN REVIEWED THE CAMPED V CORPS IN AND AROUND THIS FIELD.

Four Years of Civil War

I have just read your despatch about sore tongued and fatigued horses. Will you pardon me for asking what the horses of your army have done since the battle of Antietam that fatigue anything?

DISPATCH TO GENERAL GEORGE MCCLELLAN, OCTOBER 24, 1862

ABOVE: PRESIDENT LINCOLN LIKELY SAW THE SUNKEN ROAD, ALSO KNOWN AS BLOODY LANE, AN AREA OF INTENSE FIGHTING, WHILE TOURING THE BATTLEFIELD AFTER THE BATTLE OF ANTIETAM. THERE WERE MORE CASUALTIES IN ONE DAY AT ANTIETAM THAN IN ANY OTHER BATTLE IN AMERICAN HISTORY.

RIGHT: ABRAHAM LINCOLN VISITED THE DUNKARD CHURCH WHILE TOURING THE ANTIETAM BATTLEFIELD, ANTIETAM NATIONAL BATTLEFIELD, NEAR SHARPSBURG, MARYLAND. THE CHURCH BECAME A FIELD HOSPITAL DURING THE BATTLE.

You remember my speaking to you of what I called your over-cautiousness. Are you not over-cautious when you assume that you can not do what the enemy is constantly doing? Should you not claim to be at least his equal in prowess, and act upon the claim? . . . You know I desired, but did not order, you to cross the Potomac below, instead of above the Shenandoah and Blue Ridge. My idea was that this would at once menace the enemies' communications, which I would seize if he would permit. If he should move Northward I would follow him closely, holding his communications. If he should prevent our seizing his communications, and move towards Richmond, I would press closely to him, fight him if a favorable opportunity should present, and, at least, try to beat him to Richmond on the inside track. I say "try"; if we never try, we shall never succeed. DISPATCH TO GENERAL GEORGE McCLELLAN, OCTOBER 13, 1862

Lincoln reviewed twelve divisions. The troops were glad to have the President among them. One soldier observed that as Lincoln reviewed the ranks on October 3, his "kindly smile . . . touched the hearts of the bronzed, rough-looking men more than one can express. It was like an electric shock. It flew from elbow to elbow; and, with one loud cheer which made the air ring, the suppressed feeling gave vent, conveying to the good President that his smile had gone home, and found a ready response." A trooper wrote that "[w]e marched proudly away, for we all felt proud to know that we had been permitted to see and salute him." Several soldiers noted that Lincoln "looked careworn and sorrowful." One thought the President appeared "much more careworn" than he seemed in his pictures, so much so that it seemed as if "one of his feet is in the grave."

He has been three times hit, — twice at Antietam with but slight injury, and once very severly at Fredericksburg. Also has had two horses shot under him.

MEMORANDUM CONCERNING PROMOTION OF COLONEL JOSEPH SNIDER, MARCH 9, 1863

During his stay with the army, Lincoln visited hospitals, including one which housed some Confederates. To them he remarked "that if they had no objection he would be pleased to take them by the hand" and that "the solemn obligations which we owe to our country and posterity compel the prosecution of this war, and it followed that many were our enemies through uncontrollable circumstances, and he bore them no malice, and could take them by the hand with sympathy and good feeling." The Confederates, after a brief silence, "came forward, and each silently but fervently shook the hand of the President." He then approached those too seriously wounded to stand and "bid them to be of good cheer; assuring them that every possible care should be bestowed upon them to ameliorate their condition." There was not a dry eye in the hospital.

WINTER WHEAT GROWS AT THE PRY HOUSE WHERE PRESIDENT LINCOLN VISITED WOUNDED GENERAL ISRAEL RICHARDSON. THE HOME IS NOW THE PRY HOUSE FIELD HOSPITAL MUSEUM, PART OF THE NATIONAL MUSEUM OF CIVIL WAR MEDICINE WITHIN ANTIETAM NATIONAL BATTLEFIELD.

May our children and our children's children to a thousand generations, continue to enjoy the benefits conferred upon us by a united country, and have cause yet to rejoice under those glorious institutions bequeathed us by Washington and his compeers.

SPEECH AT RAILROAD STATION, FREDERICK, MARYLAND, OCTOBER 4, 1862

LINCOLN LIKELY CROSSED THE BURNSIDE BRIDGE, AN AREA OF HEAVY FIGHTING, WHILE TOURING THE BATTLEFIELD WITH GENERAL GEORGE McCLELLAN AT ANTIETAM NATIONAL BATTLEFIELD, NEAR SHARPSBURG, MARYLAND.

Four Years of Civil War

In giving freedom to the slave, we assure freedom to the free—honorable alike in what we give, and what we preserve. We shall nobly save, or meanly lose, the last best, hope of earth. Other means may succeed; this could not fail. The way is plain, peaceful, generous, just—a way which, if followed, the world will forever applaud, and God must forever bless.

ANNUAL MESSAGE TO CONGRESS, DECEMBER 1, 1862

THE NORTH ENTRANCE OF THE WHITE HOUSE—NO CONFIRMED PHOTOGRAPHS OF ABRAHAM LINCOLN STANDING OUTSIDE THE WHITE HOUSE EXIST, BUT A PHOTOGRAPH OF HIS SON THOMAS, NICKNAMED TAD, WAS MADE STANDING HERE IN FRONT OF THE WHITE HOUSE. (NATIONAL HISTORIC LANDMARK)

I am very little inclined on any occasion to say anything unless I hope to produce some good by it.   ADDRESS TO UNION MEETING AT WASHINGTON, D.C., AUGUST 6, 1862

...all persons held as slaves within any State or designated part of a State, the people whereof shall then be in rebellion against the United States, shall be then, thenceforward, and forever free; and the Executive Government of the United States, including the military and naval authority thereof, will recognize and maintain the freedom of such persons, and will do no act or acts to repress such persons, or any of them, in any efforts they may make for their actual freedom.   EMANCIPATION PROCLAMATION, JANUARY 1, 1863

The White House failed to impress Lincoln's secretaries, who disparaged its "threadbare appearance" and referred to it as "a dirty rickety concern." The north side of the Executive Mansion, facing Pennsylvania Avenue, was marred by an immense portico that seemed to dwarf the building, and the statue of Thomas Jefferson on the lawn before the front entrance was a green, moldy eyesore.

Passing beneath the outsized portico, visitors entered the front door, passed through a small lobby, then entered a large vestibule, where coat racks were set up for large public receptions. Those events were held in the enormous East Room, which had "a faded, worn, untidy look" and needed fresh paint and new furniture.

Three other state parlors, designated by their colors, were smaller. Beyond these three parlors was the modestly-appointed state dining room, which could accommodate up to thirty-five dinner guests. A smaller family dining room adjoined it on the north side. On the far end of the west wing was a spacious conservatory. A massive staircase led to the second floor, which housed offices as well as the family quarters.

THE NORTH SIDE OF THE WHITE HOUSE FROM PENNSYLVANIA AVENUE, WASHINGTON, D.C.

Four Years of Civil War

There is no doubt that Gen. Meade, now commanding the Army of the Potomac, beat Lee, at Gettysburg, Pa. at the end of a three days battle; and that the latter is now crossing the Potomac at Williamsport, over the swolen stream & with poor means of crossing, and closely pressed by Meade. We also have despatches rendering it entirely certain that Vicksburg surrendered to Gen. Grant on the glorious old 4th.

LETTER TO FREDERICK F. LOW, JULY 8, 1863

VIEW FROM A CONFEDERATE BATTERY OF BIG ROUND TOP TO THE LEFT AND BUSHMAN HILL TO THE RIGHT
AT GETTYSBURG NATIONAL MILITARY PARK, PENNSYLVANIA.

Again, my dear general, I do not believe you appreciate the magnitude of the misfortune involved in Lee's escape. He was within your easy grasp, and to have closed upon him would, in connection with our other late successes, have ended the war. As it is, the war will be prolonged indefinitely. If you could not safely attack Lee last monday, how can you possibly do so South of the river, when you can take with you very few more than two thirds of the force you then had in hand? It would be unreasonable to expect, and I do not expect you can now effect much. Your golden opportunity is gone, and I am distressed immeasureably because of it.

LETTER TO GENERAL GEORGE MEADE, JULY 14, 1863

In June 1863, elements of Robert E. Lee's Confederate army converged on the small town of Gettysburg, Pennsylvania. There, during the first three days of July, the bloodiest battle of the war was fought. Lee lost fully a third of his men (28,000) while the Union commander, George G. Meade, lost a fifth of his (23,000). The Union Army, occupying high ground, fended off repeated attacks, including the fabled charge of George Pickett's division on July 3. The following day, Lee's shattered army began retreating toward the Potomac. Word of the victory filled Lincoln's heart with joy, though Meade's order congratulating his troops did not. That general said their job was now to "drive from our soil every vestige of the presence of the invader." When Lincoln read this proclamation, his heart sank. A friend saw that an "expression of disappointment settled upon his face" and that "his hands dropped on his knees." In "tones of anguish" the President exclaimed: "Drive the invader from our soil! My God! Is that all?" Lincoln called it "a dreadful reminiscences of McClellan. The same spirit that moved McClellan to claim a great victory because Pennsylvania and Maryland were safe." Exasperated, he asked: "Will our Generals never get that idea out of their heads? The whole country is our soil."

A CONFEDERATE BATTERY IN THE FOG BEFORE DAWN ON SEMINARY RIDGE AT THE CENTER OF PICKETT'S CHARGE, GETTYSBURG NATIONAL MILITARY PARK, PENNSYLVANIA.

FOUR YEARS OF CIVIL WAR

Now we are engaged in a great civil war, testing whether that nation, or any nation so conceived and so dedicated, can long endure.

GETTYSBURG ADDRESS, NOVEMBER 19, 1863

THE GETTYSBURG RAILROAD STATION WHERE PRESIDENT LINCOLN ARRIVED AND DEPARTED GETTYSBURG, PENNSYLVANIA, FOR THE DEDICATION OF THE GETTYSBURG NATIONAL CEMETERY. UNDER STEWARDSHIP OF THE NATIONAL TRUST FOR HISTORIC GETTYSBURG, THE RAILROAD STATION IS NOW A MUSEUM.

In the summer of 1863, David Wills, an aggressive and successful young attorney in Gettysburg, organized an effort to create a national cemetery for the Union soldiers killed there. Wills and his fellow planners decided to consecrate the site with a solemn ceremony and invited Lincoln to deliver "a few appropriate remarks" at that event. On November 18, Lincoln traveled to Gettysburg and spent the night at Wills's home. After dinner, serenaders regaled him there. One of them recalled that the "appearance of the President was the signal for an outburst of enthusiasm that I had never heard equaled. When the people cheered and otherwise expressed their delight, he stood before us bowing his acknowledgments." He then asked to be excused from addressing them: "I appear before you, fellow-citizens, merely to thank you for this compliment. The inference is a very fair one that you would like to hear me for a little while at least, were I to commence to make a speech. I do not appear before you for the purpose of doing so, and for several substantial reasons. The most substantial of these is that I have no speech to make. [Laughter.] In my position it is somewhat important that I should not say any foolish things." An irreverent voice rang out: "If you can help it." Lincoln replied good-naturedly: "It very often happens that the only way to help it is to say nothing at all. [Laughter.] Believing that is my present condition this evening, I must beg of you to excuse me from addressing you further." The crowd greeted these remarks with "a tremendous outburst of applause."

THE DAVID WILLS HOUSE IS WHERE PRESIDENT LINCOLN STAYED WHILE MAKING FINAL PREPARATIONS FOR DELIVERING THE GETTYSBURG ADDRESS AT THE DEDICATION FOR THE NEW SOLDIERS' NATIONAL CEMETERY, GETTYSBURG, PENNSYLVANIA. THE DAVID WILLS HOUSE AND MUSEUM ARE PART OF GETTYSBURG NATIONAL MILITARY PARK.

FOUR YEARS OF CIVIL WAR

We have come to dedicate a portion of that field, as a final resting place for those who here gave their lives that that nation might live. GETTYSBURG ADDRESS, NOVEMBER 19, 1863

November 19 at Gettysburg was, as Lincoln's assistant personal secretary John Hay reported, "one of the most beautiful Indian Summer days ever enjoyed." As people swarmed into the little town, Lincoln rose early, toured the battlefield, and polished his address. At 10 a.m. he joined the procession to the cemetery, led by his friend Ward Hill Lamon, the marshal in charge of arrangements. Upon emerging from the Wills house, wearing a black suit and white gauntlets, Lincoln encountered a huge crowd which greeted him with "enthusiastic and long continued cheers," causing him to blush. His admirers insisted on shaking hands until the marshals finally intervened to protect his arm from more wrenching.

A journalist noted that Lincoln's "awkwardness which is so often remarked does not extend to his horsemanship." Other reporters wrote that once he had mounted "a splendid black horse," Lincoln "sat up the tallest and grandest rider in the procession, bowing and nearly laughing his acknowledgments to the oft-repeated cheers – 'Hurrah for Old Abe;' and 'We're coming, Father Abraham,' and one solitary greeting of its kind, 'God save Abraham Lincoln.'" In a letter written by a Gettysburg resident ten days after the event, the President was described as "gracefully bowing with a modest smile and uncovered head to the throng of women, men and children that greeted him from the doors and windows." The writer added that even though Lincoln appeared "cheerful and happy on that day, an observant eye could see that the dreadful responsibility that this nation and this wicked rebellion has cast upon him has had its marked effect, and that he feels the terrible responsibility that rests upon him."

ABOVE: THE GATEHOUSE AT EVERGREEN CEMETERY IN GETTYSBURG IN THE WARM, FIRST LIGHT OF MORNING. ABRAHAM LINCOLN DELIVERED THE GETTYSBURG ADDRESS A SHORT WALK FROM THE GATEHOUSE.

PREVIOUS LEFT: THE BLACK IRON FENCE SEPARATING EVERGREEN CEMETERY AND GETTYSBURG NATIONAL CEMETERY IS THE SAME FENCE THAT SURROUNDED THE WHITE HOUSE WHEN ABRAHAM LINCOLN WAS PRESIDENT.

PREVIOUS RIGHT: THIS ICONIC PORTRAIT OF PRESIDENT LINCOLN WAS MADE BY ALEXANDER GARDNER IN WASHINGTON, D.C., ON NOVEMBER 8, 1863, ELEVEN DAYS BEFORE HE DELIVERED THE GETTYSBURG ADDRESS AT THIS LOCATION.

Four Years of Civil War

It is rather for us to be here dedicated to the great task remaining before us—that from these honored dead we take increased devotion to that cause for which they gave the last full measure of devotion . . . GETTYSBURG ADDRESS, NOVEMBER 19, 1863

THE SUN COMES UP JUST LEFT OF LITTLE ROUND TOP AT GETTYSBURG NATIONAL MILITARY PARK, PENNSYLVANIA.
SEVERAL AREAS THAT SAW INTENSIVE FIGHTING CAN BE SEEN FROM BEHIND THIS CONFEDERATE BATTERY
ON WARFIELD RIDGE NEAR THE EMMITSBURG ROAD.

Four score and seven years ago our fathers brought forth on this continent, a new nation, conceived in Liberty, and dedicated to the proposition that all men are created equal.

Now we are engaged in a great civil war, testing whether that nation, or any nation so conceived and so dedicated, can long endure. We are met on a great battle-field of that war. We have come to dedicate a portion of that field, as a final resting place for those who here gave their lives that that nation might live. It is altogether fitting and proper that we should do this.

But, in a larger sense, we can not dedicate—we can not consecrate—we can not hallow—this ground. The brave men, living and dead, who struggled here, have consecrated it, far above our poor power to add or detract. The world will little note, nor long remember what we say here, but it can never forget what they did here. It is for us the living, rather, to be dedicated here to the unfinished work which they who fought here have thus far so nobly advanced. It is rather for us to be here dedicated to the great task remaining before us—that from these honored dead we take increased devotion to that cause for which they gave the last full measure of devotion—that we here highly resolve that these dead shall not have died in vain—that this nation, under God, shall have a new birth of freedom—and that government of the people, by the people, for the people, shall not perish from the earth.

GETTYSBURG ADDRESS, NOVEMBER 19, 1863

THE GETTYSBURG ADDRESS IS THE MOST WELL-KNOWN SPEECH IN UNITED STATES HISTORY.
EDWARD EVERETT WAS REGARDED AS THE LEADING ORATOR OF THE ANTEBELLUM AND CIVIL WAR ERA. LINCOLN'S ADDRESS FOLLOWED A TWO-HOUR ORATION BY EVERETT, THE FEATURED SPEAKER AT THE DEDICATION CEREMONY OF THE GETTYSBURG NATIONAL CEMETERY. THE FOLLOWING DAY, EVERETT WROTE LINCOLN, "PERMIT ME ALSO TO EXPRESS MY GREAT ADMIRATION OF THE THOUGHTS EXPRESSED BY YOU, WITH SUCH ELOQUENT SIMPLICITY & APPROPRIATENESS, AT THE CONSECRATION OF THE CEMETERY. I SHOULD BE GLAD, IF I COULD FLATTER MYSELF THAT I CAME AS NEAR TO THE CENTRAL IDEA OF THE OCCASION, IN TWO HOURS, AS YOU DID IN TWO MINUTES."

Four Years of Civil War

It is easy to see that, under the sharp discipline of civil war, the nation is beginning a new life.

Annual Message to Congress, December 8, 1863

The White House in the twilight after dusk. (National Historic Landmark)

I am constantly pressed by those who scold before they think, or without thinking at all . . . LETTER TO MAJOR GENERAL JOHN McCLERNAND, AUGUST 12, 1863

Back in Washington after his trip to Gettysburg, Lincoln came down with a mild case of smallpox, known as varioloid, which persisted for several days. Part of that time he was quarantined. When told that his illness was contagious, he quipped "that since he has been President he had always had a crowd of people asking him to give them something, but that now he has something he can give them all." Alluding to both the scars that smallpox often caused and to his own appearance, he told his physician: "There is one consolation about the matter, doctor. It cannot in the least disfigure me!"

The varioloid did more than disfigure one of the members of the presidential party at Gettysburg, William H. Johnson, the young black man who accompanied Lincoln from Illinois and served in The White House until his fellow black staffers there objected to his presence because his skin was too dark. Lincoln then obtained for him a job in the treasury department. Johnson contracted smallpox, which killed him in January 1864. One day that month, as Johnson lay in the hospital, a journalist discovered the President counting out some greenbacks. Lincoln explained that such activity "is something out of my usual line, but a President of the United States has a multiplicity of duties not specified in the Constitution or acts of Congress. This is one of them. This money belongs to a poor Negro [Johnson] who is a porter in one of the departments (the Treasury) and who is at present very bad with the smallpox. He did not catch it from me, however; at least I think not. He is now in hospital and could not draw his pay because he could not sign his name. I have been at considerable trouble to overcome the difficulty and get it for him and have at length succeeded in cutting red tape. I am now dividing the money and putting by a portion labeled, in an envelope, with my own hands, according to his wish." When Johnson died, Lincoln paid for his funeral and arranged to have him buried in Arlington National Cemetery, where his gravestone (which Lincoln also paid for) reads simply: "William Johnson, Citizen."

FOUR YEARS OF CIVIL WAR

Tell Tad the goats and father are very well—especially the goats.

TELEGRAM TO MARY TODD LINCOLN, APRIL 28, 1864

THE NORTH PORTICO OF THE WHITE HOUSE, WASHINGTON, D.C., LATE IN THE AFTERNOON OF EARLY SUMMER.
PUBLIC ACCESS AND SECURITY WERE MUCH DIFFERENT WHEN ABRAHAM LINCOLN WAS PRESIDENT. THE EXECUTIVE MANSION
WAS OFTEN OPEN TO THE PUBLIC AND LINCOLN TOLERATED A CONSTANT ANNOYANCE OF VISITORS WITH REQUESTS AND ADVICE.
(NATIONAL HISTORIC LANDMARK)

On the east side of the second floor of The White House was the President's sparsely-furnished office, which a presidential secretary described as "a wonderful historic cavern" with "less space for the transaction of the business of his office than a well-to-do New York lawyer." In the middle of the room stood a long table around which the Cabinet sat. By the center window overlooking the Potomac was Lincoln's upright desk, resembling something from a used furniture auction. Maps were displayed on racks in a corner of the room, a portrait of Andrew Jackson hung above the fireplace, and a large photograph of the English reformer John Bright adorned one wall. Adjoining this office-cum-cabinet-meeting-chamber was a large waiting room, through which Lincoln had to pass in order to reach the living area. (The only modification to the house made during his presidency was a partition installed toward the rear of the waiting room, creating a private passageway from the office to the family quarters). Those quarters included an oval library-cum-family-room which was, as a presidential secretary put it, "a really delightful retreat." In addition to bedrooms for the President and First Lady, there were four others, one of which was for Willie and Tad.

PRESIDENT LINCOLN'S PERSONAL OFFICE AND CABINET ROOM WAS ON THE SECOND FLOOR OF THE WHITE HOUSE.
NOW KNOWN AS THE LINCOLN BEDROOM, ONE OF ITS TWO WINDOWS CAN BE SEEN TO THE FAR RIGHT.

Let us diligently apply the means, never doubting that a just God, in his own good time, will give us the rightful result.

LETTER TO JAMES C. CONKLING, AUGUST 26, 1863

And while it has not pleased the Almighty to bless us with a return of peace, we can but press on, guided by the best light He gives us, trusting that in His own good time, and wise way, all will yet be well.

ANNUAL MESSAGE TO CONGRESS, DECEMBER 1, 1862

On Sundays, Lincoln often attended services at the nearby New York Avenue Presbyterian Church, where the Rev. Dr. Phineas Gurley presided. Upon arriving in Washington, the President asked friends and allies for recommendations for a church to attend. "I wish to find a church," he said, "whose clergyman holds himself aloof from politics." At first, his young sons Willie and Tad went to Sunday school there, but later the headstrong Tad revolted, preferring to go to the livelier Fourth Presbyterian Church where his friends Holly and Bud Taft and their family worshipped.

Four days after Lincoln died, Gurley delivered the funeral sermon at The White House in which he remarked: "Since the days of Washington, no man was ever so deeply and firmly imbedded and enshrined in the hearts of the people, as Abraham Lincoln; nor was it a mistaken confidence and love. He deserves it all. He merited by his character, by his acts, and by the whole tone and tenor of his life. His integrity was thorough, all pervading, all controlling, and incorruptible. He saw his duty as the chief magistrate of a great and imperilled people, and he determined to do his duty, seeking the guidance and leaning on the arm of Him of Whom it is written: 'He giveth to the faint, and to them who have no Might he increaseth strength.' Never shall I forget the emphatic and deep emotion with which he said, in this very room to a company of clergymen who had called to pay their respect to him in the darkest days of the civil conflict. 'Gentlemen, my hope of success in this struggle rests on that immutable foundation, the justice and goodness of God, and when events are very threatening, I still hope that in some way all will be well in the end, because our cause is just and God will be on our side.'"

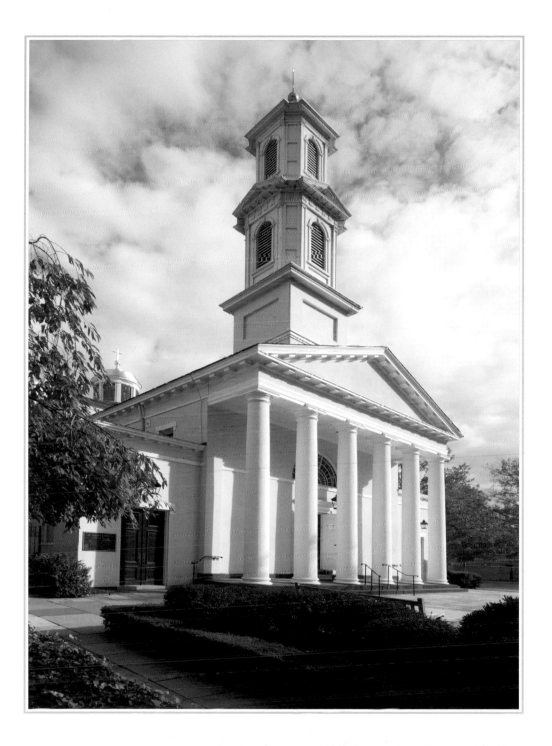

Located conveniently across from The White House, St. John's Episcopal Church was long known as "the church of the presidents." Lincoln first attended services there the day after he arrived in Washington. A journalist reported: "Mr. Lincoln was dressed in plain black clothes, with black whiskers and hair well trimmed, and was pronounced by such as recognized him as a different man entirely from the hard-looking pictorial representations seen of him. Some of the ladies say he is almost good looking."

ABOVE: SAINT JOHN'S EPISCOPAL CHURCH ON LAFAYETTE SQUARE, WASHINGTON, D.C. BEGINNING WITH JAMES MADISON, EVERY PRESIDENT HAS ATTENDED SERVICES HERE ON AT LEAST ONE OCCASION, GIVING THE CHURCH THE TITLE, "CHURCH OF THE PRESIDENTS." (NATIONAL HISTORIC LANDMARK)

PREVIOUS PAGE: THE NEW YORK AVENUE PRESBYTERIAN CHURCH IN WASHINGTON, D.C., FREQUENTLY ATTENDED BY ABRAHAM AND MARY LINCOLN.

It is hard to say that anything has been more bravely, and well done, than at Antietam, Murfreesboro, Gettysburg, and on many fields of lesser note.

LETTER TO JAMES C. CONKLING, AUGUST 26, 1863

I am naturally anti-slavery. If slavery is not wrong, nothing is wrong. I can not remember when I did not so think, and feel. And yet I have never understood that the Presidency conferred upon me an unrestricted right to act officially upon this judgment and feeling.

LETTER TO ALBERT G. HODGES, APRIL 4, 1864

In July 1864, Confederate General Jubal Early menaced Washington, coming within a few hundred feet of Fort Stevens, three miles north of The White House. On July 11, eager to observe the action first-hand, Lincoln hastened to that fort. As he gazed at the skirmishing from the parapet, a soldier rudely instructed him to get down lest he be shot. He did so. Excited, Lincoln returned to the War Department and vividly described the action. That evening he was in an exceptionally good mood. The next day he revisited Fort Stevens, accompanied this time by his wife. As he again watched the action from the parapet, an army surgeon standing nearby was shot in the thigh. At the urging of General Horatio Wright, Lincoln descended from his exposed perch.

As Early withdrew, Lincoln thought the Union forces should "push right up the river road & cut off as many as possible of the retreating raiders." Though he urged General Henry Halleck to see that it was done, the Confederates managed to slip across the Potomac unmolested, to the President's visible disgust. Sarcastically, he remarked that General Horatio Wright had halted his pursuit and "sent out an infantry reconnaissance, for fear he might come across the rebels and catch some of them." Lincoln often cited Early's escape as one of the most exasperating developments of the war. He had predicted a day before Early entered Maryland on his way to Washington that "with decent management" Union forces could "destroy any enemy who crosses the Potomac."

Above: Abraham Lincoln personally observed the Battle of Fort Stevens on July 11 and 12, 1864, a battle at one of the encircling forts protecting Washington, D.C. Lincoln came under fire from Confederate sharpshooters two days in a row at the battle, while an army surgeon was shot next to him.

Previous Page: This portrait of Abraham Lincoln was made by Anthony Berger at the Mathew Brady Gallery in Washington, D.C. on February 9, 1864.

FOUR YEARS OF CIVIL WAR

We start to you at One P.M. to-day. May lie over during the dark hours of the night. Very small party of us.

I send this over as a reminder in relation to allowing the "Thomas Colyer" to run between here & Mount-Vernon.

I have seen your despatch expressing your unwillingness to break your hold where you are. Neither am I willing. Hold on with a bull-dog gripe, and chew & choke, as much as possible.

On April 9, 1865, Lincoln and some companions were returning to Washington from a visit to the Virginia front. As they sailed by Mount Vernon, a friend predicted to Lincoln that Americans would one day revere his home in Springfield as much as they did George Washington's home. "Springfield! How happy, four years hence, will I be to return there in peace and tranquility!" the President exclaimed. (A few days earlier, when John Todd Stuart, his first law partner, had asked him if he intended to return to the Illinois capital after his presidency, Lincoln replied: "Mary does not expect ever to go back there, and don't want to go – but I do – I expect to go back and make my home in Springfield for the rest of my life.")

ABRAHAM LINCOLN TRAVELED PAST MOUNT VERNON BY STEAMBOAT ON TRIPS UP AND DOWN THE POTOMAC RIVER OVER A PERIOD OF SEVERAL YEARS. IN 1862, LINCOLN'S SHIP DOCKED AT MOUNT VERNON, BUT IT IS UNCERTAIN IF HE VISITED THE ESTATE OR WASHINGTON'S TOMB, GEORGE WASHINGTON'S MOUNT VERNON ESTATE AND GARDENS, VIRGINIA. (NATIONAL HISTORIC LANDMARK)

The view from Mount Vernon directly across the Potomac River to Piscataway Park, operated by the National Park Service, looks much as it did when Washington and Lincoln looked across this land.

Four Years of Civil War

Last night at 10.15, when it was dark as a rainy night without a moon could be, a furious cannonade, soon joined in by a heavy musketry-fire, opened near Petersburg and lasted about two hours. The sound was very distinct here, as also were the flashes of the guns upon the clouds. It seemed to me a great battle . . . TELEGRAM TO SECY. OF WAR EDWIN STANTON, MARCH 30, 186.

ABOVE: ABRAHAM LINCOLN WENT TO MEET GENERAL ULYSSES S. GRANT AT GRANT'S HEADQUARTERS IN CITY POINT
ON THE ST. JAMES RIVER NEAR PETERSBURG TO ENSURE A PLAN TO LEAD TO THE END OF THE WAR,
GRANT'S CABIN AT CITY POINT, PETERSBURG NATIONAL BATTLEFIELD, VIRGINIA.

FOLLOWING PAGE: PRESIDENT LINCOLN MET GENERAL GRANT IN PETERSBURG AT THE THOMAS WALLACE HOUSE ON APRIL 3, 1865,
GRANT'S TEMPORARY HEADQUARTERS AFTER THE FALL OF PETERSBURG. WALLACE INVITED LINCOLN
INSIDE THE HOUSE, BUT HE STAYED ON THE PORCH TO CONSULT WITH GENERAL GRANT.

Upon arriving in Petersburg, Lincoln rode down the largely deserted streets to Grant's headquarters. The President's face was "radiant and joyful" as he grabbed the general's hand, which he shook for a long while as he poured from his overflowing heart profound thanks and congratulations. It was one of the happiest moments of his life. "The scene was singularly affecting, and one never to be forgotten," recalled one of Grant's aides.

Lincoln said: "Do you know, general, I had a sort of sneaking idea all along that you intended to do something like this; but I thought some time ago that you would so maneuver as to have Sherman come up and be near enough to cooperate with you."

"Yes," replied Grant, "I thought at one time that Sherman's army might advance far enough to be in supporting distance of the Eastern armies when the spring campaign against Lee opened; but I had a feeling that it would be better to let Lee's old antagonists give his army the final blow, and finish up the job. If the Western troops were even to put in an appearance against Lee's army, it might give some of our politicians a chance to stir up sectional feeling in claiming everything for the troops from their own section of the country. The Western armies have been very successful in their campaigns, and it is due to the Eastern armies to let them vanquish their old enemy single-handed."

Lincoln then discussed postwar political arrangements, emphasizing that he wished the Rebels would be treated leniently. After about an hour and a half, Grant returned to the front. En route back to the train station, Lincoln passed by numerous houses demolished by artillery fire. He paused before the remains of the Dunlop Mansion, which had been struck over 100 times, and shook his head. As he rode along, troops greeted Lincoln jocularly, shouting out, "How are you, Abe?" and "Hello, Abe!" Upon returning to City Point, he was refreshed and energized, happily convinced that the war would soon end.

Four Years of Civil War

I repeat this now. If Jefferson Davis wishes, for himself, or for the benefit of his friends at the North, to know what I would do if he were to offer peace and re-union, saying nothing about slavery, let him try me.   LETTER TO CHARLES D. ROBINSON, AUGUST 17, 1864

FOLLOWING THE SURRENDER OF RICHMOND, PRESIDENT LINCOLN VISITED THE CONFEDERATE EXECUTIVE MANSION,
THE JEFFERSON DAVIS RESIDENCE, IN RICHMOND, VIRGINIA. THE MANSION IS ALSO CALLED
THE WHITE HOUSE OF THE CONFEDERACY. (NATIONAL HISTORIC LANDMARK)

This morning Gen. Grant reports Petersburg evacuated; and he is confident Richmond also is. He is pushing forward to cut off if possible, the retreating army. I start to him in a few minutes.

TELEGRAM TO SECRETARY OF WAR EDWIN STANTON, APRIL 3—8:00 A.M., 1865

Thanks for your caution; but I have already been to Petersburg, staid with Gen. Grant an hour & a half and returned here. It is certain now that Richmond is in our hands, and I think I will go there to-morrow.
I will take care of myself.   TELEGRAM TO SECRETARY OF WAR EDWIN STANTON, APRIL 3—5:00 P.M., 1865

If you can find, any person anywhere professing to have any proposition of Jefferson Davis in writing, for peace, embracing the restoration of the Union and abandonment of slavery, what ever else it embraces, say to him he may come to me with you, and that if he really brings such proposition, he shall, at the least, have safe conduct, with the paper (and without publicity, if he choose) to the point where you shall have met him.   LETTER TO HORACE GREELEY, JULY 9, 1864

Entering Richmond on April 4, the day after the Confederates abandoned it, Lincoln called on the Union commander, who was occupying the Confederate White House. There Lincoln, looking "pale and haggard" and "utterly worn out with fatigue and the excitement of the past hour," sat down in Jefferson Davis's chair and softly requested a glass of water. An observer noted that there "was no triumph in his gesture or attitude. He lay back in the chair like a tired man whose nerves had carried him beyond his strength." He wore a "look of unutterable weariness, as if his spirit, energy and animating force were wholly exhausted," a journalist reported. So tired was he that when he stepped onto the balcony to acknowledge the cheering crowd in the street, he merely bowed rather than speaking.

THE PORTICO ON THE SOUTH SIDE OF THE CONFEDERATE EXECUTIVE MANSION, THE JEFFERSON DAVIS RESIDENCE.

Four Years of Civil War

... I think I will go there to-morrow. Telegram to Secretary of War Edwin Stanton, April 3, 1865

They formally entered into a treaty of temporary alliance, and co-operation with the so-called "Confederate States," and sent members to their Congress at Montgomery. And, finally, they permitted the insurrectionary government to be transferred to their capital at Richmond. The people of Virginia have thus allowed this giant insurrection to make its nest within her borders; and this government has no choice left but to deal with it, where it finds it.

Message to Congress in special session, July 4, 1861

In Richmond's Capitol Square, Lincoln allegedly addressed a huge, mostly black crowd. According to Admiral David Dixon Porter, the President said: "My poor friends, you are free – free as air. You can cast off the name of slave and trample upon it; it will come to you no more. Liberty is your birthright. God gave it to you as he gave it to others, and it is a sin that you have been deprived of it for so many years. But you must try to deserve this priceless boon. Let the world see that you merit it, and are able to maintain it by your good works. Don't let your joy carry you into excesses. Learn the laws and obey them; obey God's commandments and thank him for giving you liberty, for to him you owe all things. There, now, let me pass on; I have but little time to spare. I want to see the capital, and must return at once to Washington to secure to you that liberty which you seem to prize so highly."

Lincoln then toured the capitol, which the legislators had precipitously abandoned two days earlier. Overturned desks, bundles of Confederate money, and random government documents were strewn about haphazardly.

President Lincoln would have seen the George Washington Equestrian Monument on April 4, 1865, when he visited the Virginia State Capitol on the Capitol Square, Richmond, Virginia.

PRESIDENT LINCOLN VISITED THE VIRGINIA STATE CAPITOL, WHICH SERVED AS THE CAPITOL OF THE CONFEDERACY,
AFTER THE SURRENDER OF RICHMOND, VIRGINIA. THE STATE CAPITOL BUILDING IS THE SECOND OLDEST IN THE UNITED STATES.
(NATIONAL HISTORIC LANDMARK)

ROBERT E. LEE'S CONFEDERATE ARMY SURRENDERED TO GENERAL ULYSSES S. GRANT ON APRIL 9, 1865. PRESIDENT LINCOLN WAS RELIEVED THAT THE END OF THE WAR HAD FINALLY COME, YET WAS STILL VERY BUSY AS PRESIDENT. FIVE DAYS LATER, THE ASSASSINATION OF ABRAHAM LINCOLN OCCURRED, FORD'S THEATRE NATIONAL HISTORIC SITE, WASHINGTON, D.C.

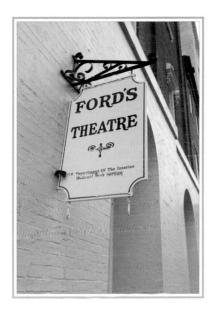

We meet this evening, not in sorrow, but in gladness of heart. The evacuation of Petersburg and Richmond, and the surrender of the principal insurgent army, give hope of a righteous and speedy peace whose joyous expression can not be restrained. In the midst of this, however, He, from Whom all blessings flow, must not be forgotten. A call for a national thanksgiving is being prepared, and will be duly promulgated. Nor must those whose harder part gives us the cause of rejoicing, be overlooked. Their honors must not be parcelled out with others. I myself, was near the front, and had the high pleasure of transmitting much of the good news to you; but no part of the honor, for plan or execution, is mine. To Gen. Grant, his skilful officers, and brave men, all belongs.

LAST PUBLIC ADDRESS, APRIL 11, 1865

Around 8:30 p.m. on April 14, as Lincoln prepared to leave The White House, he asked his son Robert if he would like to come along. Robert declined, citing fatigue. So the President and First Lady climbed into their carriage and proceeded to pick up Major Henry R. Rathbone and his stepsister (who was also his fiancée) Clara Harris. When General Grant and his wife announced that they could not join the presidential party, Mrs. Lincoln had invited the young couple to do so. The First Lady called Miss Harris a "dear friend." Together the two women often took carriage rides and, according to Miss Harris, she regularly attended plays with the Lincolns. The party reached Ford's Theatre about half an hour after the curtain had risen on Tom Taylor's light comedy, "Our American Cousin." As they entered, the orchestra struck up "Hail to the Chief," and the audience rose to greet them with vociferous applause, which Lincoln acknowledged with a smile and bow. As he moved toward the box, he looked to one observer "mournful and sad."

THE SIGN IN FRONT OF FORD'S THEATRE NATIONAL HISTORIC SITE IN WASHINGTON, D.C.

The Long Struggle is Over

In the midst of this, however, He, from Whom all blessings flow, must not be forgotten.

Last public address, April 11, 1865

On April 14 (Good Friday), when John Wilkes Booth heard that Grant and the President would attend Ford's Theatre that night, he impulsively decided to kill them. Earlier he had mentioned the possibility of murdering the President, but not to his colleagues in the plot to capture Lincoln, which had fizzled the previous month. Summoning the remnants of the kidnapping team (David Herold, George Atzerodt, and Lewis Powell), Booth assigned them various tasks. Powell was to kill Secretary of State William Henry Seward, Atzerodt was to kill Vice-President Andrew Johnson, and Herold was to assist Booth's escape after he shot Lincoln. The murder of Johnson and Seward would heighten the effect of the presidential assassination, throwing the government into chaos.

Booth's motives are not entirely clear, but he was an avid white supremacist whose racist rage formed an important part of his psyche. Indignation at the proposal that blacks would become citizen-voters prompted him to act. (Booth had responded to Lincoln's April 11 speech — in which the President called for limited black suffrage — by vowing: "That means nigger citizenship. Now by God I'll put him through!" Thus Lincoln was a martyr to black civil rights, as much as Martin Luther King, Jr. and other activists who fell victim to racist violence a century later.

THE PRESIDENTIAL BOX WHERE THE LINCOLNS WERE SITTING TO WATCH "OUR AMERICAN COUSIN",
FORD'S THEATRE NATIONAL HISTORIC SITE IN WASHINGTON, D.C.

I am glad of this interview, and glad to know that I have your sympathy and prayers. We are indeed going through a great trial—a fiery trial. In the very responsible position in which I happen to be placed, being a humble instrument in the hands of our Heavenly Father, as I am, and as we all are, to work out his great purposes, I have desired that all my works and acts may be according to his will, and that it might be so, I have sought his aid—but if after endeavoring to do my best in the light which he affords me, I find my efforts fail, I must believe that for some purpose unknown to me, He wills it otherwise If I had had my way, this war would never have been commenced; If I had been allowed my way this war would have been ended before this, but we find it still continues; and we must believe that He permits it for some wise purpose of his own, mysterious and unknown to us; and though with our limited understandings we may not be able to comprehend it, yet we cannot but believe, that he who made the world still governs it.

REPLY TO ELIZA P. GURNEY, OCTOBER 26, 1862

THE PETERSEN HOUSE, THE BOARDING HOUSE WHERE ABRAHAM LINCOLN DIED THE FOLLOWING MORNING IS ACROSS THE STREET FROM FORD'S THEATRE, FORD'S THEATRF NATIONAL HISTORIC SITE, WASHINGTON, D.C.

TRIBUTES FROM A NATION

Every man is said to have his peculiar ambition. Whether it be true or not, I can say for one that I have no other so great as that of being truly esteemed of my fellow men, by rendering myself worthy of their esteem. How far I shall succeed in gratifying this ambition . . .

FIRST CAMPAIGN ANNOUNCEMENT IN SANGAMO JOURNAL, NEW SALEM, MARCH 9, 1832

In late April, a train carried Lincoln's body from Washington to Springfield. At several cities en route, the coffin was displayed for public viewing. A Philadelphia newspaper reported that a "grand, emphatic and unmistakable tribute of affectionate devotion to the memory of our martyred chief was that paid by Philadelphia on the arrival of his remains. . . . No mere love of excitement, no idle curiosity to witness a splendid pageant, but a feeling far deeper, more earnest, and founded in infinitely nobler sentiments, must have inspired that throng, which, like the multitudinous waves of the swelling sea, surged along our streets from every quarter of the city, gathering in a dense, impenetrable mass along the route prescribed for the procession. . . . The myriads of expectant faces gathering around the depot . . . and lining the route of the procession for hours before the arrival of the funeral train; the various civic associations marching in orderly column, with banners draped in mourning, to take their assigned places; the bands leading such associations, and making the city vocal with strains sweet but melancholy; the folds of sable drapery drooping from the buildings, and the half-masted flags, with their mourning borders; all were striving to express the same emotion. . . . Never before in the history of our city was such a dense mass of humanity huddled together. Hundreds of persons were seriously injured from being pressed in the mob, and many fainting females were extricated by the police and military and conveyed to places of security. Many women lost their bonnets, while others had nearly every particle of clothing torn from their persons. Notwithstanding the immense pressure and the trying ordeal through which persons had to pass in order to view the remains, but little disorder prevailed, every one apparently being deeply impressed with the great solemnity of the occasion. After a person was once in line, it took from four to five hours before an entrance into the Hall [Independence Hall] could be effected. Spectators were not allowed to stop by the side of the coffin, but were kept moving on, the great demand on the outside not permitting more than a mere glance at the remains, which were under military guard." Similar demonstrations of widespread, profound grief took place at Baltimore, Harrisburg, New York, Albany, Buffalo, Cleveland, Columbus, Indianapolis, Chicago, and Springfield.

... I am exceedingly anxious that this Union, the Constitution, and the liberties of the people shall be perpetuated in accordance with the original idea for which that struggle was made, and I shall be most happy indeed if I shall be an humble instrument in the hands of the Almighty, and of this, his almost chosen people, for perpetuating the object of that great struggle.

ADDRESS TO THE NEW JERSEY SENATE EN ROUTE TO THE WHITE HOUSE, FEBRUARY 21, 1861

LINCOLN TOMB STATE HISTORIC SITE IN SPRINGFIELD, ILLINOIS, WHERE ALL OF ABRAHAM LINCOLN'S FAMILY IS BURIED, EXCEPT ROBERT WHO IS BURIED AT ARLINGTON NATIONAL CEMETERY. (NATIONAL HISTORIC LANDMARK)

TRIBUTES FROM A NATION

The Almighty has His own purposes. SECOND INAUGURAL ADDRESS, MARCH 4, 1865

ABOVE: THE TWILIGHT BEFORE DAWN SHINES IN THE REFLECTING POOL AT THE LINCOLN MEMORIAL NATIONAL MEMORIAL, WASHINGTON, D.C. SINCE ITS CREATION, THE MEMORIAL DRAWS PEOPLE WHO ASSOCIATE LINCOLN WITH INTEGRITY AND JUSTICE.

RIGHT: THE ICONIC SCULPTURE OF PRESIDENT LINCOLN AT THE LINCOLN MEMORIAL NATIONAL MEMORIAL, WASHINGTON, D.C.

Every one likes a compliment. Thank you for yours on my little notification speech, and on the recent Inaugural Address. I expect the latter to wear as well as—perhaps better than—any thing I have produced; but I believe it is not immediately popular. Men are not flattered by being shown that there has been a difference of purpose between the Almighty and them. To deny it, however, in this case, is to deny that there is a God governing the world. It is a truth which I thought needed to be told; and as whatever of humiliation there is in it, falls most directly on myself, I thought others might afford for me to tell it.

LETTER TO THURLOW WEED, MARCH 15, 1865

The Lincoln Memorial, which stands at the far end of Washington's National Mall, is a classical Doric temple, designed by Henry Bacon. It houses a massive, nineteen-foot-tall statue of Lincoln, the work of sculptor Daniel Chester French, who is also renowned for such iconic works as the Minute Man at Concord, Massachusetts. In 1911, Congress authorized construction of the memorial, which was dedicated in 1922. Carved into the wall above the huge seated figure of Lincoln is a simple statement: "In this temple, as in the hearts of the people for whom he saved the Union, the memory of Abraham Lincoln is enshrined forever." On the side walls of the interior are carved the full texts of the Gettysburg Address and the Second Inaugural, Lincoln's greatest prose masterpieces.

In 1963, another famous speech was delivered at the memorial: Martin Luther King, Jr.'s "I Have a Dream," given during the March on Washington for Jobs and Freedom.

Fellow Countrymen

At this second appearing to take the oath of the presidential office, there is less occasion for an extended address than there was at the first. Then a statement, somewhat in detail, of a course to be pursued, seemed fitting and proper. Now, at the expiration of four years, during which public declarations have been constantly called forth on every point and phase of the great contest which still absorbs the attention, and engrosses the energies of the nation, little that is new could be presented. The progress of our arms, upon which all else chiefly depends, is as well known to the public as to myself; and it is, I trust, reasonably satisfactory and encouraging to all. With high hope for the future, no prediction in regard to it is ventured.

On the occasion corresponding to this four years ago, all thoughts were anxiously directed to an impending civil-war. All dreaded it—all sought to avert it. While the inaugeral address was being delivered from this place, devoted altogether to saving the Union without war, insurgent agents were in the city seeking to destroy it without war—seeking to dissolve the Union, and divide effects, by negotiation. Both parties deprecated war; but one of them would make war rather than let the nation survive; and the other would accept war rather than let it perish. And the war came.

One eighth of the whole population were colored slaves, not distributed generally over the Union, but localized in the Southern part of it. These slaves constituted a peculiar and powerful interest. All knew that this interest was, somehow, the cause of the war. To strengthen, perpetuate, and extend this interest was the object for which the insurgents would rend the Union, even by war; while the government claimed no right to do more than to restrict the territorial enlargement of it. Neither party expected for the war, the magnitude, or the duration, which it has already attained. Neither anticipated that the cause of the conflict might cease with, or even

254

before, the conflict itself should cease. Each looked for an easier triumph, and a result less fundamental and astounding. Both read the same Bible, and pray to the same God; and each invokes His aid against the other. It may seem strange that any men should dare to ask a just God's assistance in wringing their bread from the sweat of other men's faces; but let us judge not that we be not judged. The prayers of both could not be answered; that of neither has been answered fully. The Almighty has His own purposes. "Woe unto the world because of offences! for it must needs be that offences come; but woe to that man by whom the offence cometh!" If we shall suppose that American Slavery is one of those offences which, in the providence of God, must needs come, but which, having continued through His appointed time, He now wills to remove, and that He gives to both North and South, this terrible war, as the woe due to those by whom the offence came, shall we discern therein any departure from those divine attributes which the believers in a Living God always ascribe to Him? Fondly do we hope—fervently do we pray—that this mighty scourge of war may speedily pass away. Yet, if God wills that it continue, until all the wealth piled by the bond-man's two hundred and fifty years of unrequited toil shall be sunk, and until every drop of blood drawn with the lash, shall be paid by another drawn with the sword, as was said three thousand years ago, so still it must be said "the judgments of the Lord, are true and righteous altogether."

With malice toward none; with charity for all; with firmness in the right, as God gives us to see the right, let us strive on to finish the work we are in; to bind up the nation's wounds; to care for him who shall have borne the battle, and for his widow, and his orphan—to do all which may achieve and cherish a just, and a lasting peace, among ourselves, and with all nations.

SECOND INAUGURAL ADDRESS, MARCH 4, 1865

TRIBUTES FROM A NATION

Even my little speech, shows how this was; and if you will go to the Library you may get the Journals of 1845-6, in which you can find the whole for yourself.

LETTER TO WILLIAM H. HERNDON, JUNE 22, 1848

Besides this, our friends there had provided a magnificent flag of the country. They had arranged it so that I was given the honor of raising it to the head of its staff; and when it went up, I was pleased that it went to its place by the strength of my own feeble arm. When, according to the arrangement, the cord was pulled and it flaunted gloriously to the wind without an accident, in the bright glowing sun-shine of the morning, I could not help hoping that there was in the entire success of that beautiful ceremony, at least something of an omen of what is to come. Nor could I help, feeling then as I often have felt, that in the whole of that proceeding I was a very humble instrument.

ADDRESS TO THE PENNSYLVANIA GENERAL ASSEMBLY AT HARRISBURG, FEBRUARY 22, 1861

Situated in the heart of downtown Springfield, Illinois, the Abraham Lincoln Presidential Library and Museum complex consists of three buildings: the museum, the adjacent library, and the nearby visitors center, located in the former Springfield train station. The library opened in 2004 and the museum the following year. In the immediate neighborhood are other important Lincoln sites, including the Old State Capitol, where Lincoln served as a legislator and where he gave his "House Divided" speech in 1858, and the Lincoln-Herndon Law Offices. A few blocks away are the Lincoln Home, where the Lincolns lived from 1844 to 1861, and the First Presbyterian Church, where they often attended worship services.

THE ABRAHAM LINCOLN PRESIDENTIAL LIBRARY AND MUSEUM ON A LATE AFTERNOON IN AUGUST.

THE ABRAHAM LINCOLN PRESIDENTIAL LIBRARY AND MUSEUM AT DUSK IN MAY,
A SHORT WALK FROM MANY LOCATIONS WHERE LINCOLN MADE HISTORY.

Epilogue

When Lincoln died, of the many eulogists who paid tribute to his memory, none was more eloquent than Frederick Douglass, who addressed a large audience at Manhattan's Cooper Union on June 1, 1865: "No people or class of people in the country," he declared, "have a better reason for lamenting the death of Abraham Lincoln, and for desiring to honor and perpetuate his memory, than have the colored people." The record of the martyred President, when compared "with the long line of his predecessors, many of whom were merely the facile and servile instruments of the slave power," was impressive. Douglass acknowledged that Lincoln was "unsurpassed in his devotion to the welfare of the white race," and that "he sometimes smote" blacks "and wounded them severely;" nevertheless he was also "in a sense hitherto without example, emphatically the black man's President: the first to show any respect for their rights as men. . . . He was the first American President who . . . rose above the prejudice of his times, and country." If during the early stages of the Civil War the President had favored colonizing the freedmen abroad, Douglass asserted, "Lincoln soon outgrew his colonization ideas and schemes and came to look upon the Black man as an American citizen." To illustrate this point, Douglass cited his personal experience: "It was my privilege to know Abraham Lincoln and to know him well. I saw and conversed with him at different times during his administration." Douglass found Lincoln's willingness to receive him remarkable in itself: "He knew that he could do nothing which would call down upon him more fiercely the ribaldry of the vulgar than by showing any respect to a colored man." (In a draft of this speech, Douglass said: "Some men there are who can face death and dangers, but have not the moral courage to contradict a prejudice or face ridicule. In daring to admit, nay in daring to invite a Negro to an audience at the White house, Mr. Lincoln did that which he knew would be offensive to the crowd and excite their ribaldry. It was saying to the country, I am President of the black people as well as the white, and I mean to respect their rights and feelings as men and as citizens.")

When Douglass was admitted to the President's office, he found him easy to talk with: "He set me at perfect liberty to state where I differed from him as freely as where I agreed with him. From the first five minutes I seemed to myself to have been acquainted with [him] during all my life . . . [H]e was one of the very few white Americans who could converse with a Negro without anything like condescension, and without in anywise reminding him of the unpopularity of his color."

Douglass recalled one episode in particular that demonstrated Lincoln's "kindly disposition towards colored people." While Douglass was talking with the President, a White House aide on two occasions announced that the Governor of Connecticut sat in an adjacent room, eager for an interview. "Tell the Governor to wait," said the President. "I want to have a long talk with my friend Douglass." Their conversation continued for another hour. Douglass later speculated that "[t]his was probably the first time in the history of the country when the governor of a state was required to wait for an interview, because the President of the United States was engaged in conversation with a negro."

Douglass did not rely solely on his own experience to explain why Lincoln should be considered "emphatically the black man's President." He told the Cooper Union audience about "[o]ne of the most touching scenes connected with the funeral of our lamented President," which "occurred at the gate of the Presidential Mansion: A colored woman standing at the gate weeping, was asked the cause of her tears. 'Oh! Sir,' she said, 'we have lost our Moses.' 'But,' said the gentleman, 'the Lord will send you another;' 'That may be,' said the weeping woman, 'but Ah! we had him.'"

But Lincoln speaks to us as more than a champion of black freedom, or of democracy, or of national unity. He is also an ongoing source of inspiration. Few people will achieve his world historical importance, but many can profit from his personal example, encouraged by the knowledge that despite a childhood of emotional malnutrition and grinding poverty, despite a lack of formal education, despite a series of career failures, despite a miserable marriage, despite a tendency to depression, despite a painful midlife crisis, despite the early death of his mother and his siblings as well as of his sweetheart and two of his four children, he became a model of psychological maturity, moral clarity, and unimpeachable integrity. His presence and his leadership inspired his contemporaries; his life story can do the same for generations to come.

Michael Burlingame

THE HILL-MCNEIL STORE IN A HEAVY FOG AT SUNRISE, LINCOLN'S NEW SALEM STATE HISTORIC SITE.

Abraham Lincoln Historic Sites

Kentucky
Abraham Lincoln Birthplace National Historic Site - Hodgenville
Lincoln's Boyhood Home Unit at Knob Creek (part of Abraham Lincoln Birthplace N.H.S.) - near Hodgenville
Farmington Historic Plantation - Louisville

Indiana
Lincoln Boyhood National Memorial - Spencer County, Lincoln City (National Historic Landmark)
Lincoln Ferry Park - near Troy
Colonel William Jones State Historic Site - Gentryville

Illinois
Lincoln Trail Homestead State Memorial - near Decatur
Lincoln's New Salem State Historic Site - near Petersburg
Apple River Fort State Historic Site - Elizabeth
Kellogg's Grove: Black Hawk Battlefield Park - near Kent
Colonel Matthew Rogers Building: Long Nine Museum - Athens
Vandalia Statehouse State Historic Site - Vandalia
Lincoln Home National Historic Site - Springfield (National Historic Landmark)
Lincoln-Herndon Law Offices State Historic Site - Springfield
Old State Capitol State Historic Site - Springfield (National Historic Landmark)
Edwards Place Historic Home: Springfield Art Association - Springfield
Elijah Iles House - Springfield
Illinois Executive Mansion - Springfield
Middletown Stagecoach Inn - Middletown
Metamora Courthouse State Historic Site - Metamora
David Davis Mansion State Historic Site - Bloomington (National Historic Landmark)
Miller-Davis Buildings: David Davis Law Office - Bloomington
Postville Courthouse State Historic Site - Lincoln
Mount Pulaski Courthouse State Historic Site - Mount Pulaski
C.H. Moore Law Office - Clinton
Lincoln Trail Road - Champaign County
William Fithian Home: Vermilion County Museum - Danville
Lincoln Log Cabin State Historic Site - near Lerna
Rueben Moore Home (part of Lincoln Log Cabin State Historic Site) - near Lerna
Taylorville Courthouse: Christian County Historical Museum - Taylorville
Ratcliff Inn Museum - Carmi
John Shastid House: The Pike County Historical Museum - Pittsfield
Beardstown Courthouse: Old Lincoln Courtroom & Museum - Beardstown
Archer House - Marshall (National Historic Landmark)
Mt. Vernon Appellate Courthouse - Mt. Vernon
DeSoto House Hotel - Galena
Bryant Cottage State Historical Site - Bement
Old Main at Knox College - Galesburg (National Historic Landmark)
St. James Cathedral - Chicago

VACHEL LINDSAY HOME STATE HISTORIC SITE - SPRINGFIELD (NATIONAL HISTORIC LANDMARK)
GREAT WESTERN RAILROAD STATION - SPRINGFIELD
LINCOLN TOMB STATE HISTORIC SITE - SPRINGFIELD (NATIONAL HISTORIC LANDMARK)

WISCONSIN
TALLMAN HOUSE: ROCK COUNTY HISTORICAL SOCIETY - JANESVILLE

NEW YORK
NIAGARA FALLS STATE PARK (NATIONAL HISTORIC LANDMARK)
THE GREAT HALL OF THE COOPER UNION - NEW YORK CITY (NATIONAL HISTORIC LANDMARK)

NEW HAMPSHIRE
PHILLIPS EXETER ACADEMY - EXETER
EXETER TOWN HALL - EXETER
FOLSOM BLOCK BOARDING HOUSE - EXETER

DISTRICT OF COLUMBIA
UNITED STATES CAPITOL - WASHINGTON, D.C. (NATIONAL HISTORIC LANDMARK)
THE WHITE HOUSE - WASHINGTON, D.C. (NATIONAL HISTORIC LANDMARK)
PRESIDENT LINCOLN'S COTTAGE AT THE SOLDIERS' HOME NATIONAL MONUMENT - WASHINGTON, D.C.
        (NATIONAL HISTORIC LANDMARK)
SMITHSONIAN CASTLE: SMITHSONIAN INSTITUTION - WASHINGTON, D.C. (NATIONAL HISTORIC LANDMARK)
SAINT JOHN'S CHURCH - LAFAYETTE SQUARE, WASHINGTON, D.C. (NATIONAL HISTORIC LANDMARK)
NEW YORK AVENUE PRESBYTERIAN CHURCH - WASHINGTON, D.C.
FORT STEVENS BATTLEFIELD NATIONAL PARK - WASHINGTON, D.C.
FORD'S THEATRE NATIONAL HISTORIC SITE - WASHINGTON, D.C.
PETERSEN HOUSE (PART OF FORD'S THEATRE NATIONAL HISTORIC SITE) - WASHINGTON, D.C.
LINCOLN MEMORIAL NATIONAL MEMORIAL - WASHINGTON, D.C.

VIRGINIA
GREAT FALLS NATIONAL PARK - MCLEAN
CHATHAM MANOR: FREDERICKSBURG NATIONAL MILITARY PARK - FREDERICKSBURG
GEORGE WASHINGTON'S MOUNT VERNON ESTATE AND GARDENS - NEAR ALEXANDRIA (NATIONAL HISTORIC LANDMARK)
GRANT'S CABIN AT CITY POINT: PETERSBURG NATIONAL BATTLEFIELD - PETERSBURG
WHITE HOUSE OF THE CONFEDERACY - RICHMOND (NATIONAL HISTORIC LANDMARK)
VIRGINIA STATE CAPITOL - RICHMOND (NATIONAL HISTORIC LANDMARK)

WEST VIRGINIA
HARPERS FERRY NATIONAL HISTORIC PARK - HARPERS FERRY

MARYLAND
ANTIETAM NATIONAL BATTLEFIELD - SHARPSBURG
PRY HOUSE FIELD HOSPITAL MUSEUM (PART OF ANTIETAM NATIONAL BATTLEFIELD) - SHARPSBURG

Pennsylvania
Gettysburg National Military Park - Gettysburg
Gettysburg Railroad Station - Gettysburg
David Wills House (Gettysburg National Military Park) - Gettysburg
Evergreen Cemetery Gatehouse - Gettysburg

70 Lincoln Historic Sites Included
Kentucky - 3
Indiana - 3
Illinois - 36
Wisconsin - 1
New York - 2
New Hampshire - 3
Washington, D.C. - 10
Virginia - 6
West Virginia - 1
Maryland - 1
Pennsylvania - 4

Included here are 3 National Historic Sites, 2 National Memorials, 1 National Monument, and several parks and other locations administered by the National Park Service. There are 14 State Historic Sites and 1 State Memorial. 18 Lincoln historic sites are designated National Historic Landmarks.

16 historic sites and museums listed here are dedicated exclusively to the historical heritage of Abraham Lincoln. Many other historical sites have been preserved in large degree because of the 150 years of admiration for our 16th President, his integrity and accomplishments.

A great deal of gratitude goes to the private owners who have worked to preserve several of the Lincoln historic sites listed here. Also, to all the volunteers who work at many of the Lincoln sites, giving of their time to educate visitors—making very special places. This is a great tribute.

The Abraham Lincoln Presidential Library and Museum in the twilight after dusk.

This portrait of Abraham Lincoln was made by Alexander Gardner at his studio in Washington, D.C. on February 5, 1865. The portrait was one of several made in Lincoln's last formal portrait session, all revealing a smile on Lincoln's face following the passage of the Thirteenth Amendment to the United States Constitution through congress several days before.

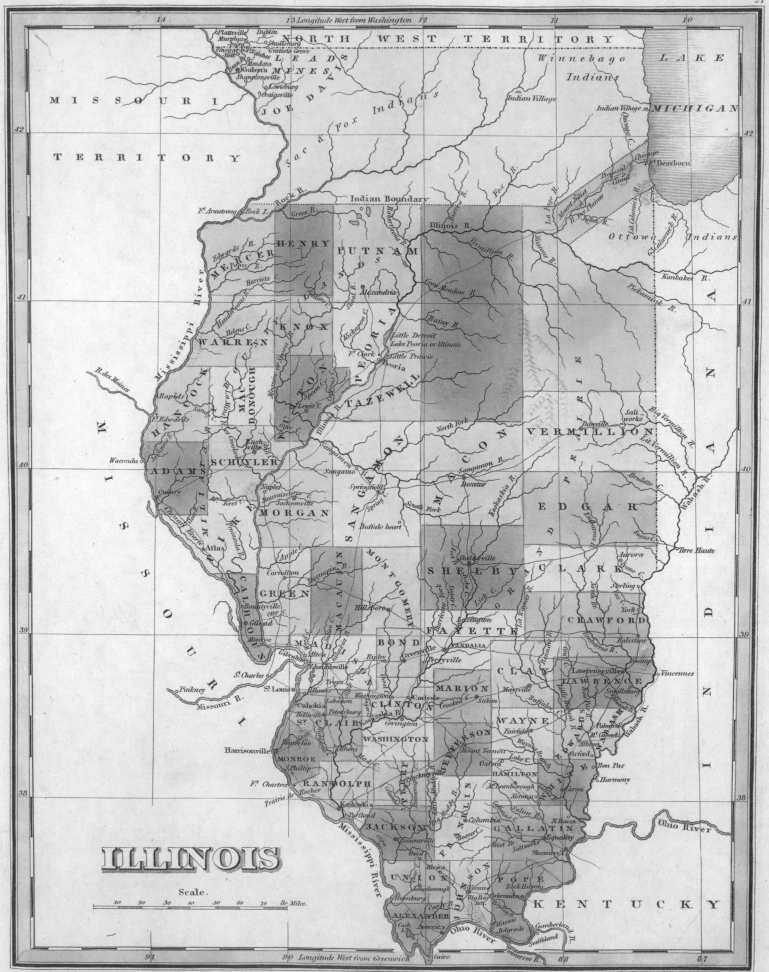

ILLINOIS

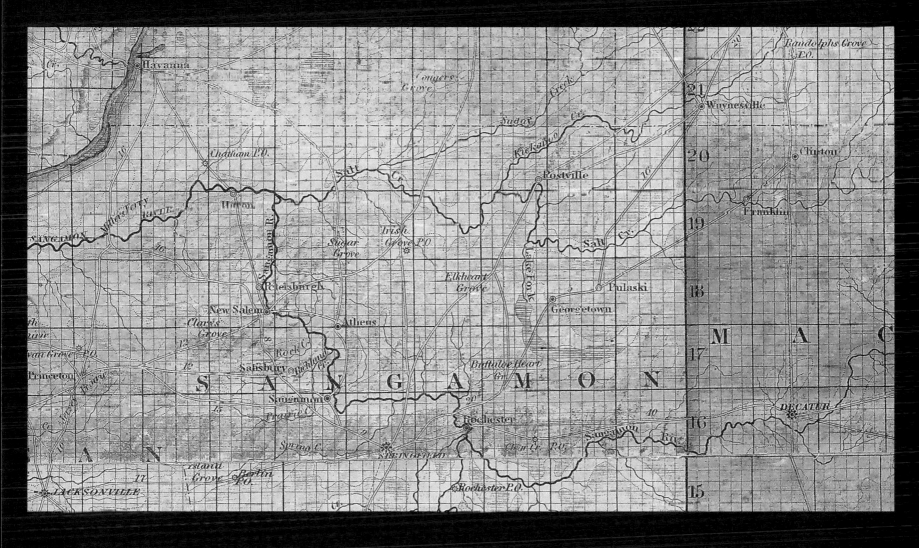

New Salem 1836

Above: Map showing New Salem in 1836, Lincoln's fifth year living in the village.
(New Sectional Map of the State of Illinois by J.M. Peck and John Messinger,
published by J.H. Colton & Co.)

Illinois 1831

Previous page: Map of Illinois in 1831, the year Abraham Lincoln left his parent's homestead
near Decatur and moved to New Salem.
(A New General Atlas published in 1831 by Anthony Finley)

United States 1860

Following pages: Map of the United States in 1860, the year Abraham Lincoln was elected
President. This is the structure of the country at the beginning of the Civil War. In 1863,
Lincoln issued a proclamation admitting West Virginia to the Union after it separated from
Virginia. Lincoln proclaimed Nevada a state in 1864.
(Mitchell's New General Atlas published in 1860 by Samuel Augustus Mitchell, Jr.)

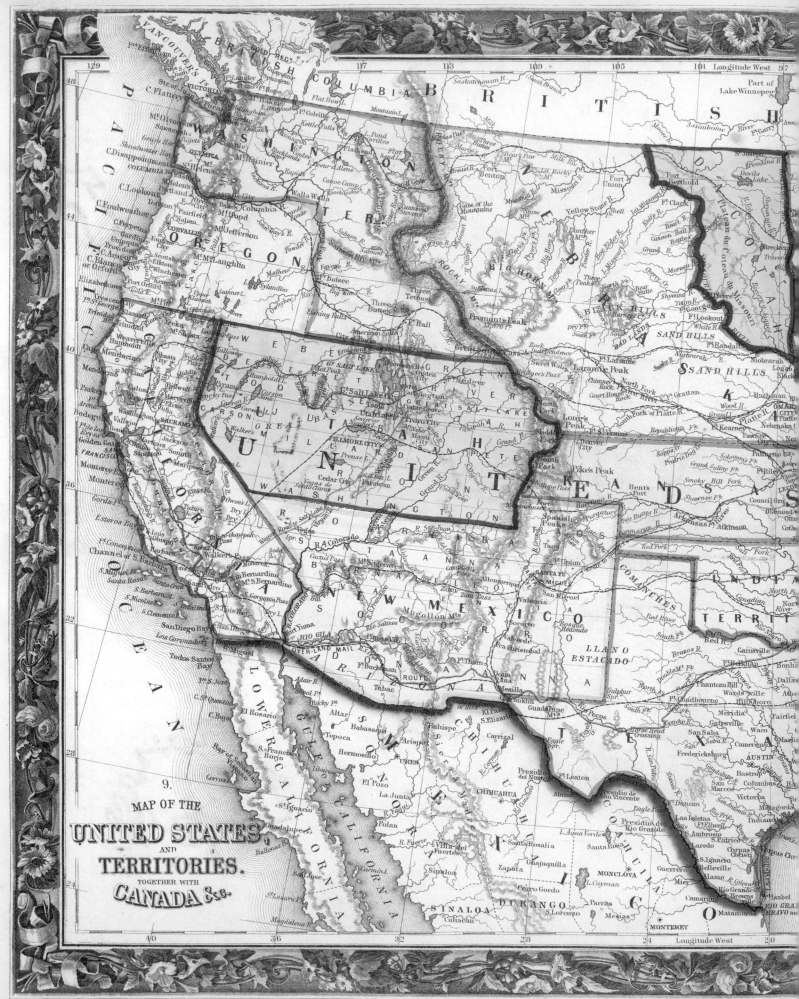

9.

MAP OF THE
UNITED STATES,
AND
TERRITORIES.
TOGETHER WITH
CANADA &c.

Abraham Lincoln Traveled This Way — The America Lincoln Knew

Photography, concept, and book design by Robert Shaw
Narrative and Epilogue by Michael Burlingame
Preface and captions by Robert Shaw
Graphics by Robert and Tricia Shaw
Editing by Carol McFeeters Thompson, Tricia Shaw, and Ann Tracy Mueller

All Abraham Lincoln writings and speeches in this book, referenced in Lincoln's handwriting, are part of the Collected Works of Abraham Lincoln, with one exception noted below. Lincoln's words are presented true to the Collected Works—quoted verbatim without indicating misspelled or missing words for visual purposes.

The Lincoln writing noted as the one exception, is a letter to Mary Todd on pages 182-184. The portion of the letter used in this book is from David Herbert Donald's book Lincoln At Home, 1999. Portions of this same letter are referenced in the Collected Works.

Paper produced, Printed and Bound 100% in the United States of America
Printed and bound by Walsworth Print Group, Marceline, Missouri
Printed on NewPage Centura Dull 100lb. Text #1 Premium
(contains 10% post-consumer recycled fiber content)

FSC
www.fsc.org
MIX
Paper from responsible sources
FSC® C004755

For information about reproduction rights of the photographs in this book
and inquiries for purchasing photographic prints, please contact:

Firelight Publishing
Post Office Box 590
Heyworth, Illinois 61745
309.473.2994   10-4PM CT, Monday-Friday
www.firelightpublishing.com
info@firelightpublishing.com

ISBN 978-1-891650-25-3
Library of Congress Control Number: 2011924996
First Edition

Dedication

To Virgil Radcliffe and William Brown—
who gave the last full measure of devotion for their country in World War II.

To Royal Cooper of the 96th Illinois Infantry Regiment, David Radcliff of the 60th Illinois Infantry Regiment, Robert Manion of the 40th Illinois Infantry Regiment, and Sidney Bagley of the 123rd Indiana Infantry Regiment, who fought in the Civil War for the Union.

Acknowledgments

Special thanks to Michael Burlingame for his brilliant, inspiring work and friendship.

Special thanks to John Warner, IV, for his generous support, friendship, and assistance with this project.

Special thanks also to the following individuals for their time and work with this project—
to Carol McFeeters Thompson for her special contribution, John Eden for his dear friendship and inspiring dedication to preserving American heritage, Tricia Shaw, Miss Savannah Shaw, Judy Shaw, Ann Tracy Mueller, Ralph Gary, Rick Schubart at Phillips Exeter Academy, and Rick McKay at The White House Photo Office.

Thanks also to Dr. Keith and Nita Kattner for their support of this project.

We would also like to thank the following individuals and organizations for their assistance:
Kent Bangert at Moore & Warner Farm Managment; Wayne Temple at the Illinois State Archives; Scott Todd; Justin Blandford at Illinois Historic Preservation Agency; Daniel Weinberg at the Abraham Lincoln Book Shop; Lawrence Jackson and Chuck Kennedy at the President Barack Obama White House Photo Office; Pat Schley, Marcia Young and Jeannie Riordan at the David Davis Mansion SHS; Bill Kemp at the McLean County Museum of History; Debra Ann Miller and Michael Krebs; Deborah Bertucci, Scott Wolfe at the DeSoto House Hotel; Tim Guinan and Jane Carrington at New Salem SHS; William Furry at the Illinois State Historical Society; Paul Beaver at Lincoln College; Winnie Golden; Phyllis Stein at the Middletown Stagecoach Inn; John Schildt; Susan Haake and David Wachtveitl at Lincoln Home NHS; Jennie Battles at the Vachel Lindsay Home SHS; Paula Woods at the Beardstown Old Lincoln Courtroom & Museum; Edward Carroll; Robert Heneghan; David Bourland at the Illinois Executive Mansion; Gary Ferguson at the Abraham Lincoln Birthplace NHS; Jane Hollenbeck Conner; Tom Huber at the Illinois State Library; David Rumsey at Cartography Associates; Helen and Stan Stites; Marian Brisard, Joey Woolridge at the Lincoln Heritage Committee of DeWitt County; Angelo Capparella and Gretchen Knapp; Loretta Vangampler at the White County Historical Society; Jill Peck; Carol Salomon at the Cooper Union; John Flood at the State of Illinois Appellate Court; Greg Langan; Mark DePue, Bryon Andreasen, James Cornelius, and Jennifer Ericson at the Abraham Lincoln Presidential Library and Museum; Susanne Wood at the Champaign County Historical Museum; Chuck Courtwright at the Christian County Historical Society and Museum; Marc and Kristie Bailey; Janis Lee and Don Nieukirk at the Tremont Museum and Historical Society; Nick Bartolomeo and the staff at Rock Creek Park; Susan Hoblit; Kathy and Kent Zimmerman at the Abe Lincoln Project of Pike County, Illinois; and Jim and Noue Filbert.

Thanks to the Abraham Lincoln Association for their work with The Collected Works of Abraham Lincoln. Also thanks to the Papers of Abraham Lincoln for their ongoing work with The Lincoln Log: A Daily Chronology of the Life of Abraham Lincoln (a project of the Illinois Historic Preservation Agency and the Abraham Lincoln Presidential Library and Museum).

About Our Underwriter

John Warner IV grew up in Clinton, Illinois where his great, great grandfather, Clifton H. Moore was the first resident attorney in DeWitt County. It was in Moore's law office in Clinton that Lincoln often worked on cases when he was in town, riding the Eighth Judicial Circuit frequently in the company of Judge David Davis. It is this very same office that John Warner has renovated and refurbished to continue as the active offices of Moore and Warner Farm Management Company.

On John Warner's father's side, his other great, great grandfather was Dr. John Warner who, as Colonel John Warner, served as a major in the 41st Illinois Volunteer Infantry from 1861 to 1865. After the war, he started an investment house called John Warner and Company that was chartered as the John Warner Bank in 1911.

Dr. Warner's son, Vespasian, served in the 20th Illinois Infantry during the Civil War, and was wounded in the battles of Shiloh and Vicksburg. Vespasian Warner subsequently married Clifton Moore's daughter and took up the practice of law with his father-in-law. Vespasian Warner and Clifton Moore both passed on stories and anecdotes of Lincoln's many visits to Clinton and DeWitt County, Illinois, recalling a number of cases that Lincoln prepared in the Moore and Warner offices.

In one such case that came before Judge David Davis's court, the Illinois Central Railroad was being sued by a farmer for damages ensuing from the construction of a right-of-way. Abraham Lincoln represented the Illinois Central and Lincoln's major political opponent, Stephen A. Douglas represented the farmer. The trial had to be postponed until the chief engineer of the Illinois Central Railroad, George B. McClellan, could come down from Chicago to testify—the very same George McClellan who, as a general in the Civil War, became the head of the Union Army.

Vespasian Warner, himself, would go on to serve as an Illinois Congressman for nearly ten years, and then would be appointed Commissioner of Pensions for Civil War veterans in President Theodore Roosevelt's administration. Having served himself in the Civil War, Vespasian took great care to make sure all who deserved a pension received their due compensation.

It was the small farming community of Clinton, Illinois that brought these prominent Civil War era leaders together and formed the rich historical legacy passed down to our sponsor, John Warner IV, by his father, and in many surviving family archival letters and documents.

We would like to give a special thanks to John Warner IV for his insight, encouragement, assistance, and generous support of this project. His partnership has made this book on Abraham Lincoln heritage possible.

Photographic Information

Abraham Lincoln traveled "a lot of ground" and spent time in numerous places in fifty-six years. With the assistance of Michael Burlingame and other dedicated historians, I attempted to reach most of the sites which still exist where good photographs could be made. It took five years and over one hundred thousand miles of travel to create the images for this book. I worked at many of the locations numerous times before I discovered the best lighting conditions, found the best seasonal conditions, and received the best weather conditions, all necessary in making the photographs needed for this collection. About a dozen of the more prominent locations were visited between twenty and thirty times each over a period of several years to capture a wide variety of seasons and visual diversity.

All the images in this book were made with Nikon digital SLR cameras and Nikkor lenses. There is no computer manipulation of skies, moons, flags, or other features in the photographs. Tripods were used for all photographs except two—one being an image made from a kayak on the Sangamon River. All photographs were made in RAW and processed using Apple Mac Pro computers with color-calibrated Apple and Eizo monitors.

Credits for Abraham Lincoln Portraits and Maps

Pages 172, 178, 187, 203, 226, 236, and 263 courtesy of the Library of Congress, Washington, D.C.
Page 214 courtesy of the National Archives, Washington, D.C.
Page 79 courtesy of the Abraham Lincoln Book Shop, Inc., Chicago, Illinois
Page 75 the Collections of The Henry Ford, Dearborn, Michigan
Page 4 courtesy of the Illinois State Historical Society, Springfield, Illinois

Maps on page 264, 266-267 courtesy of the David Rumsey Map Collection, www.davidrumsey.com
Map on page 265 the Illinois State Library, Springfield, Illinois

ROBERT SHAW IS A PROFESSIONAL LANDSCAPE PHOTOGRAPHER WHO LIVES IN THE HEART OF THE LAND OF LINCOLN. WHILE STUDYING AT ILLINOIS STATE UNIVERSITY IN 1979, SHAW DEVELOPED A PASSION FOR PHOTOGRAPHING LANDSCAPES USING FILM CAMERAS. SHAW RECEIVED DEGREES IN GEOGRAPHY, GEOLOGY, AND INDUSTRIAL TECHNOLOGY FROM ILLINOIS STATE UNIVERSITY IN 1982 AND AFTER ADDITIONAL STUDY IN PHOTOGRAPHY AND BLACK AND WHITE DARKROOM, HE BEGAN WORKING AS A PHOTOGRAPHER PROFESSIONALLY IN 1986.

OVER THE LAST 25 YEARS, ROBERT SHAW'S LANDSCAPE IMAGES FROM ACROSS THE UNITED STATES HAVE BEEN WIDELY PUBLISHED AND DISPLAYED. SHAW WORKED WITH LARGE AND MEDIUM FORMAT FILM CAMERAS FOR OVER TWENTY YEARS PRIOR TO MOVING TO DIGITAL CAMERAS. MOST LANDSCAPE IMAGES IN HIS FIRST TWO BOOKS WERE MADE WITH 4x5 VIEW CAMERAS. ALL THE IMAGES IN ABRAHAM LINCOLN TRAVELED THIS WAY WERE MADE USING HIGH RESOLUTION DIGITAL CAMERAS.

SHAW STARTED WILD PERCEPTIONS PUBLISHING, A CALENDAR AND CARD PUBLISHING COMPANY IN 1997. WILD PERCEPTIONS PRODUCES BOTH FOR NATIONAL AND REGIONAL COMPANIES, ALONG WITH CALENDARS AVAILABLE AT RETAIL STORES. SHAW ALSO PRODUCES CALENDARS AND OTHER PRINTED WORKS FOR ORGANIZATIONS, RECENTLY, A CALENDAR ENTITLED "AMERICA'S LINCOLN HERITAGE" FOR THE ABRAHAM LINCOLN PRESIDENTIAL LIBRARY & MUSEUM IN SPRINGFIELD, ILLINOIS.

SHAW'S FIRST BOOK ILLINOIS — SEASONS OF LIGHT, A COLLECTION OF NATURAL HISTORY IMAGES FROM HIS HOME STATE OF ILLINOIS, WAS PUBLISHED BY CACHE RIVER PRESS. HIS SECOND BOOK WINDY CITY WILD — CHICAGO'S NATURAL WONDERS, WAS PUBLISHED BY CHICAGO REVIEW PRESS. SHAW'S PHOTOGRAPHY HAS ALSO BEEN PUBLISHED IN BOOKS BY ABRAMS BOOKS AND NATIONAL GEOGRAPHIC BOOKS.

ROBERT SHAW'S PHOTOGRAPHY HAS BEEN FEATURED ON THE COVERS AND INSIDE "FOUR SCORE AND SEVEN" (ABRAHAM LINCOLN PRESIDENTIAL LIBRARY & MUSEUM QUARTERLY MAGAZINE), "OUTDOOR PHOTOGRAPHER", "THE NATURE CONSERVANCY", "MIDWEST STREAMS & TRAILS", "ILLINOIS AUDUBON", "ILLINOIS STEWARD" (UNIVERSITY OF ILLINOIS), "OUTDOOR ILLINOIS" (ILLINOIS DEPT. OF NATURAL RESOURCES), AND AMERICAN PARK NETWORK'S ILLINOIS STATE PARKS AND NATIONAL PARK MAGAZINES. SHAW'S PHOTOGRAPHY HAS APPEARED IN CALENDARS PUBLISHED BY AUDUBON, THE NATURE CONSERVANCY, HALLMARK, BROWN & BIGELOW, AND BROWNTROUT. SHAW'S PHOTOGRAPHY HAS BEEN USED ON CARDS PUBLISHED BY ENDURING VISIONS PUBLISHING AND WILD PERCEPTIONS. HIS PHOTOGRAPHY HAS ALSO BEEN USED BY THE FIELD MUSEUM OF NATURAL HISTORY, THE TRUST FOR PUBLIC LAND, MIDEWIN NATIONAL TALLGRASS PRAIRIE, NATIONAL CONFERENCE OF STATE LEGISLATURES, WTVP PBS AND WILL PBS, UNIVERSITY OF ILLINOIS FOUNDATION, OLD STATE CAPITOL FOUNDATION, AND THE LOOKING FOR LINCOLN HERITAGE COALITION.

Michael Burlingame is an eminent Lincoln scholar. He is the celebrated author of the biography <u>Abraham Lincoln: A Life</u>, two volumes published by Johns Hopkins University Press in 2008. He is also the author of <u>Lincoln and the Civil War</u>, published by the Southern Illinois University Press in 2011, and <u>The Inner World of Abraham Lincoln</u>, published by the University of Illinois Press in 1994. He has edited a dozen books of Lincoln primary source materials: <u>An Oral History of Abraham Lincoln: John G. Nicolay's Interviews and Essays</u>; <u>Inside Lincoln's White House: The Complete Civil War Diary of John Hay</u>; <u>Lincoln Observed: Civil War Dispatches of Noah Brooks</u>; <u>Lincoln's Journalist: John Hay's Anonymous Writings for the Press, 1860-1864</u>; <u>A Reporter's Lincoln by Walter B. Stevens</u>; <u>With Lincoln in the White House: Letters, Memoranda, and Other Writings of John G. Nicolay, 1860-1865</u>; <u>At Lincoln's Side: John Hay's Civil War Correspondence and Selected Writings</u>; <u>Inside the White House in War Times: Memoirs and Reports of Lincoln's Secretary by William O. Stoddard</u>; <u>Dispatches from Lincoln's White House: The Anonymous Civil War Journalism of Presidential Secretary William O. Stoddard</u>; <u>The Real Lincoln: A Portrait by Jesse W. Weik</u>; <u>"Lincoln's Humor" and Other Essays by Benjamin P. Thomas</u>; and <u>Abraham Lincoln: The Observations of John G. Nicolay and John Hay</u>.

Professor Burlingame was born in Washington, D.C. and attended Phillips Academy, Andover. He received his B.A. from Princeton University and his Ph.D. from Johns Hopkins University. In 1968 he joined the History Department at Connecticut College, where he taught until 2001 as the May Buckley Sadowski Professor of History Emeritus. He joined the faculty of the University of Illinois at Springfield in 2009. Professor Burlingame has received numerous awards and honors for his scholarly research and writing. He received the Abraham Lincoln Association Book Prize in 1996, the Lincoln Diploma of Honor from Lincoln Memorial University in 1998, Honorable Mention for the Lincoln Prize, Gettysburg College in 2001, and was inducted into the Lincoln Academy of Illinois in 2009. Professor Burlingame is the holder of the Chancellor Naomi B. Lynn Distinguished Chair in Lincoln Studies at the University of Illinois at Springfield.

The masterfully researched and written biography <u>Abraham Lincoln: A Life</u> won the 2010 Lincoln Prize, sponsored by the Gilder-Lehrman Institute for American History and Gettysburg College, for the finest scholarly work in English on Abraham Lincoln, or the American Civil War soldier, or a subject relating to their era. It also was a co-winner of the annual book prize awarded by the Abraham Lincoln Institute of Washington, D.C., and won the Russell P. Strange Book Award given annually by the Illinois State Historical Society for the best book on Illinois history.

A GROUP WATCHES THE SUNRISE AT THE LINCOLN MEMORIAL NATIONAL MEMORIAL, WASHINGTON, D.C. EACH COLUMN
IN THE MEMORIAL REPRESENTS ONE STATE OF THE UNION AT THE TIME OF LINCOLN'S DEATH—THE UNION LINCOLN PRESERVED.